DEVELOPING A MODEL RAILWAY
IN TT:120 SCALE

DEVELOPING A MODEL RAILWAY
IN TT:120 SCALE

DAVID ASHWOOD
&
The Market Deeping Model Railway Club, CIO

PEN & SWORD
TRANSPORT

AN IMPRINT OF PEN & SWORD BOOKS LTD.
YORKSHIRE – PHILADELPHIA

First published in Great Britain in 2025 by
Pen and Sword Transport
An imprint of
Pen & Sword Books Ltd.
Yorkshire - Philadelphia

Copyright © David Ashwood, 2025

ISBN 978 1 39903 976 5

The right of David Ashwood to be identified as author of this work has been asserted by him in accordance with the Copyright, Designs and Patents Act 1988.

A CIP catalogue record for this book is available from the British Library.

All rights reserved. No part of this book may be reproduced, transmitted, downloaded, decompiled or reverse engineered in any form or by any means, electronic or mechanical including photocopying, recording or by any information storage and retrieval system, without permission from the Publisher in writing. NO AI TRAINING: Without in any way limiting the Author's and Publisher's exclusive rights under copyright, any use of this publication to "train" generative artificial intelligence (AI) technologies to generate text is expressly prohibited. The Author and Publisher reserve all rights to license uses of this work for generative AI training and development of machine learning language models.

Typeset in 11.5/14 Palatino
by SJmagic DESIGN SERVICES, India.

The Publisher's authorised representative in the EU for product safety is Authorised Rep Compliance Ltd., Ground Floor, 71 Lower Baggot Street, Dublin D02 P593, Ireland.
www.arccompliance.com

For a complete list of Pen & Sword titles please contact

PEN & SWORD BOOKS LIMITED
George House, Beevor Street, Off Pontefract Road, Hoyle Mill,
Barnsley, South Yorkshire, England, S71 1HN.
E-mail: enquiries@pen-and-sword.co.uk
Website: www.pen-and-sword.co.uk

or

PEN AND SWORD BOOKS
1950 Lawrence Rd, Havertown, PA 19083, USA
E-mail: uspen-and-sword@casematepublishers.com
Website: www.penandswordbooks.com

Contents

Acknowledgements 7

1 Introduction 8

2 TT:120 Then and Now 12

3 The Club Challenge – *Holcombe Beach* 22

4 The Seafront 36

5 The HSTs Arrive 57

6 The Alternative Challenge – *Bluck Bridge* 63

7 The Viaduct Build 70

8 Control Options 79

9 Lighting 85

10 Buildings and Infrastructure 89

11 In Retrospect: Hornby Dublo vs TT:120 110

Acknowledgements

Our thanks to Pen & Sword Publications for taking the brave move to involve another facet of the modelling hobby beyond the military and technical. Their extensive coverage is sure to tempt anyone who has looked twice, longingly, at a museum exhibit or model kit.

Thank you also to members of the Market Deeping Club for their kind assistance and willingness to share and advise, particularly to Alan Hancock and Peter Davies for their help in reviewing and editing early drafts of this book.

All photographs are by the author unless otherwise credited.

1
Introduction

Once upon a time, to impress both change and modernity upon the public, a company had to participate in large trade fairs and expos, or produce a short film for cinematic B release. Here is the Railway Pavilion of the 1951 Festival of Britain, where the British Transport Commission showcased state of the art locomotives. To the left is 10201, a Class D16/2 1Co-Co1 2,000hp diesel built in 1950. On the right is 26020 Class 76 Bo-Bo electric locomotive of 1951, now in the national collection. The Skylon, a cigar-shaped steel tensegrity structure, can be seen framed between the two cabs. For Hornby, there were certainly trade fairs, but also in the age of the internet there was the YouTube product launch of TT:120 scale on 10 October 2022. Contemporary humour described the Skylon as being like the British economy of 1951: having no visible means of support. Perhaps unfairly, the Hornby initial product release in TT:120 garnered similar sentiments from some modellers. (*Online Transport Archive ADav-M098-3*)

It is better to have enough ideas for some of them to be wrong, than to be always right by having no ideas at all.

Edward de Bono

The Market Deeping Model Railway Club

The Market Deeping Model Railway Club (MDMRC) was formed in 1976, a year of heatwave, drought, the launch of the Chrysler Alpine and the start of the Inter-City 125 HST services from Paddington. The Club is a thriving social ecosystem of like-minded railway modellers, with a desire to learn, share, specialise and display the end result of their efforts to the public at exhibitions. Members are a wonderful mix of different careers, from professional railway people through to an ex-bank manager, computer support people and a carpenter. The Club has very much a 'can do' attitude, and a common love of building and operating railway layouts.

Unfortunately, disaster struck on the night of 17 May 2019. The Annual Model Railway Show had been set up at a school that evening in the picturesque town of Stamford, Lincolnshire, all ready for an early start the next morning. Layouts were tested and 'position one' rolling stock was in place. Traders had arrived, and their wares were set up ready to sell.

During the night a break-in took place, and a spree of vandalism occurred. Cue 6.30 am the next morning when the author and his wife, innocently expecting to make the morning's bacon rolls, opened up to discover most of the exhibits had been comprehensively reduced to matchwood. Our own layouts, those of fellow clubs, and the traders' stalls had all been demolished.

For some, 25 years of dedicated work had been destroyed, and mature tears abounded. That Saturday afternoon was spent with brooms and dustbins, and we wondered just where to go from here to offset the damage and loss of Club earnings. We decided to set up a £500 'Just Giving' request online to reduce losses.

During the following week the news was flashed around the world, seizing the common imagination. Club members appeared on television, radio and online sites. Our one operable locomotive, taken from a raffle prize, was set up on our Club's test track to show some background movement. Members of the railway modelling fraternity, wargamers, the general public, people with fond memories of their grandfathers' past showed huge sympathy, and donations poured in. From Miniatur Wonderland of Hamburg and Sir Rod

Above and overleaf: The shocking aftermath of the vandalism in 2019.

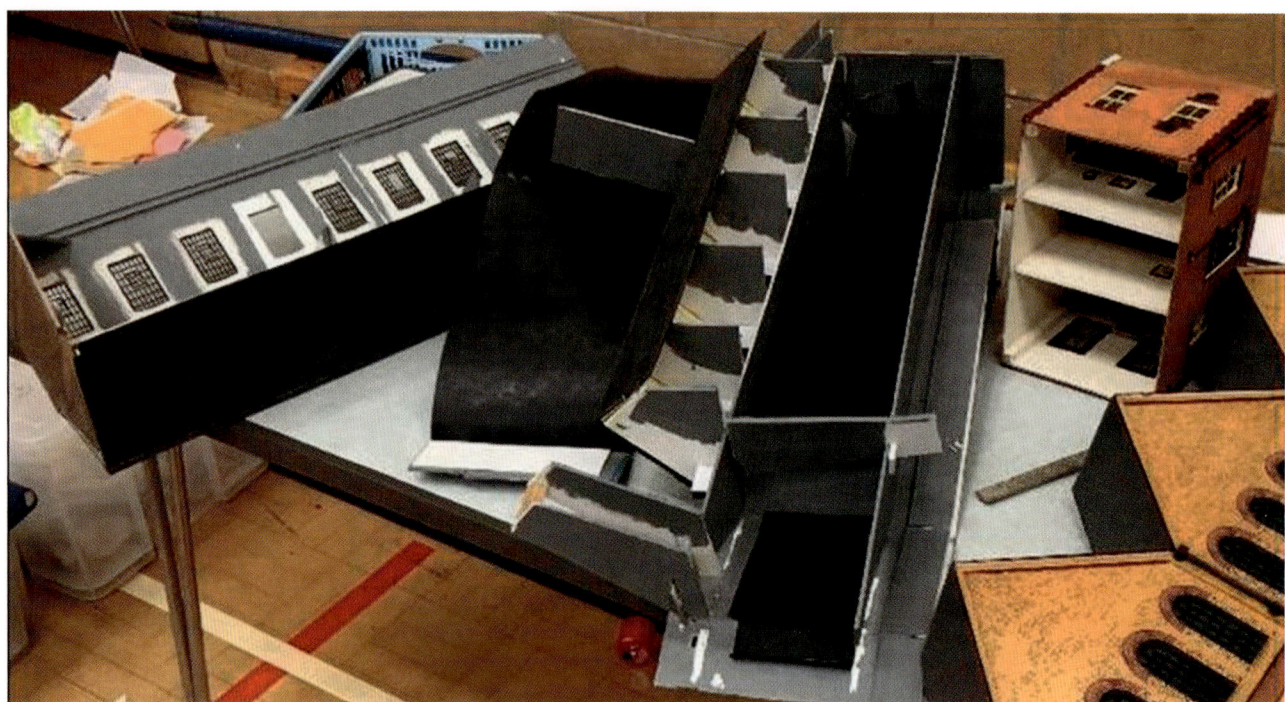

Stewart through to children's pocket money and a lady from Japan apologising for her English. It should be realised that not only the financial investment, but the time and devotion of past and older members had been utterly lost.

As a result the Club decided to reform as a charitable incorporated organisation (CIO) to process those donations appropriately, curate a historical collection of assets representing the evolution of the hobby in Britain and elsewhere, promote model clubs for local children and assist other local good causes. Good can come from bad, eventually. Our share of profits from this book goes directly back into the charity fund.

The MDMRC and TT:120

TT:120 is a scale marketed as new to the UK market, and is a true scale to gauge, since HO never really came to British outline. There was a cruder-scaled TT ('table top') product produced in the 1960s, and today there is a 3mm scale society, but until now there has been no real British outline product by a major manufacturer to match that of TT:120 in Europe and the USA.

There are many views as to why TT:120 has appeared at this time, and whether it will grow in popularity to truly rival other scales. The TT:120 rollout has been a feature of much coffee-break discussion at the Market Deeping Club.

Certainly Hornby courted controversy in the manner that the product was released and constrained, initially keeping sales just on their website, heading off market competitors with thoughts of duplicating products. Drip-feeding the range while experiencing delays to rollout dates gave a perhaps unfair sense of instability. In reality it appears that Hornby were aiming to limit risk to retailers by not offering products externally until there was an established user base. They also needed to maximise return on investment to justify expanding the range. It is unfortunate that the official TT:120 Club quickly lost a dedicated magazine. Still, the pin badge and lanyard provided are now future items of interest for collectors.

One facet of the customer base is that an older generation is returning to the hobby. They appreciate that, being a larger scale, TT:120 is easier to work with than N gauge. Options for new technology are available where needed, beyond the entry level, using the Hornby HM7000 DCC (digital command control) controller. The models certainly feel more robust than N gauge, and yet take up less space than OO. So perhaps more casual enthusiasts will be able to enter or return to the hobby, and purists will appreciate the true gauge to scale relationship. As the Hornby range grows over time, and with producers utilising the new technology of 3D printing and laser cutting, a resulting comprehensive accessory range will ensure more enthusiasts will be pulled in this direction.

If a new generation of enthusiasts is not stimulated, the hobby will shrink over time. Cab control, sound, tablet or phone, all attract the new generation. In today's smaller houses, a board that can be put under the bed for ease of use and a scale with more 'heft' than N, plus the very 'pretty' detailing on TT:120 models, will hopefully bring parents into the TT:120 train set realm, and ensure the scale has a future.

There is now a lively social media presence, an online video community and club-based exposure, all of which demonstrate that many are enjoying the challenges of expanding the limited TT:120 range. This new frontier attracts a certain personality type, which probably last flourished in the 1960s: the person who thinks, if a model or accessory does not exist yet, then how can I invent it? It can be a fun and revitalising hobby experience.

The Market Deeping Club became involved with TT:120 very early in the product's life cycle, much earlier than perhaps could be expected. This was due to a long-standing working relationship with the magazine *British Railway Modelling* (*BRM*). Previously the Club had produced a OO layout called *Amberdale*, which appeared in monthly articles. It was specifically designed to fit into a medium-sized garden shed, and was later expanded by the build team for general exhibition. Another approach to the Club from *BRM* then led us in a new direction: TT:120, and, eventually, to the writing of this book.

2
TT:120 Then and Now

Innovation can be a dirty word in railway circles. For example, the APT (Advanced Passenger Train) was derided after its press runs in 1985, and the A1A A1A 2,500hp Brown Boveri gas turbine locomotive, no. 18000 seen here at Paddington in August 1953 didn't fare much better. Nicknamed the 'Kerosene Castle' by staff, this loco is currently preserved by the Pete Waterman Trust. It was misunderstood, complex, incorrectly operated and eventually rebuilt as a test bed for other requirements. While the innovation of TT:120 from Hornby aligns with European usage of this scale, its release had a somewhat rocky start with friction against other model companies, as Hornby sought to consolidate an initial market. (*Online Transport Archive AND-M137-2*)

A comparison of scales between A3 locomotives: *Tracery* in O and *Night Hawk* in TT:120.

A Brief History of TT Scale

While innovative in its own right, TT:120 by Hornby is certainly not the first attempt at this intermediate scale (i.e. intermediate between OO and N). The TT model railway system traces its origins back to the mid twentieth century. TT scale (standing for 'table top' scale), was developed in the 1940s by Hal Joyce, an American model railroader. Joyce aimed to create a scale that was smaller than HO (1:87), which was then beginning to eclipse American O scale (1:48), allowing for more detailed models without requiring excessive space.

TT scale, with its ratio of 1:120, was officially introduced in 1945 when Hal Joyce founded the Tru-Scale company to produce model railroad equipment. The scale gained popularity in the United States, especially among enthusiasts who appreciated its balance between detail and compactness, but still occupied a tiny part of the market.

In Europe, TT scale found its foothold in Germany during the 1950s. Companies like Rokal and Zeuke (later known as Berliner TT-Bahnen and still later as Tillig) began producing TT scale model trains. They catered for a post-war imposed preference for smaller scales, due to infrastructure rebuilding often resulting in a more limited domestic space.

TT scale's popularity peaked in the 1960s and 70s, with a variety of manufacturers producing locomotives, rolling stock and accessories. However, it faced stiff competition from other scales like HO and N, which were more widely adopted.

TT scale continued to have a dedicated following, particularly in Europe where it remained relatively popular in countries such as Germany, Russia and the Czech Republic. In the United States, the scale saw a limited resurgence of interest in the 2000s among hobbyists seeking a compromise between the larger HO scale and the smaller N scale.

Today, while not as widespread as other scales, TT retains an active community of model railroaders who appreciate its unique characteristics, continue to build layouts and collect equipment. The scale's history is a testament to the enduring appeal of model

Above: Examples of Tri-ang TT wagons. Sharp but blocky injection mouldings from self-coloured plastic, with no spray painting or delicate signwriting, indicative of 1960s technology.

railroading and the diverse preferences of enthusiasts worldwide.

In the United Kingdom, 'Tri-ang TT' (or simply 'TT') was a line of model trains produced by the British company Tri-ang Railways. Tri-ang was a division of Lines Bros Ltd, a manufacturer that also produced other popular toy lines such as Tri-ang Minic and later Tri-ang Hornby.

Tri-ang TT was introduced in the late 1950s as a response to the growing popularity of model railway building in smaller scales. Again, TT scale, with a ratio of 1:101.6 or 3mm to 1ft, offered enthusiasts a compromise, this time between the larger British OO scale and N scale.

However, despite an initial success, Tri-ang TT faced challenges in the 1960s and 1970s, including increased competition from other manufacturers and shifts in consumer preferences. Lines Bros encountered financial difficulties in the late 1960s, leading to the company's eventual dissolution in 1971.

Following the closure of Lines Bros, the Tri-ang Railways brand was acquired by Hornby Railways, another prominent British model railway manufacturer. Hornby continued to produce model trains under the Tri-ang name for a period, but eventually phased out the Tri-ang TT range in favour of its own product lines.

The definition of TT is muddied somewhat by its further use as an abbreviation for 'Trix Twin', also known as 'TT-3'. The concept originated in West Germany in the early 1960s, pioneered by the Märklin company, renowned for its model trains and accessories.

Trix Twin was conceived as a way to enhance the realism and functionality of TT scale layouts by incorporating a third rail alongside the traditional two-rail configuration. This third rail, placed in the centre of the track, served as a conductor for alternating current (AC) power, while the outer two rails carried direct current (DC) power. This design allowed for more reliable electrical conductivity, smoother operation of locomotives and rolling stock, and two independently controlled locos on the same line.

Introduced in 1962, Trix Twin gained popularity among model railroaders, particularly in Europe where Märklin had a strong presence. The system offered enthusiasts the opportunity to build detailed layouts with realistic operations while still benefiting from the compact size of TT.

The Appeal of TT:120

Why might TT:120 be the ideal scale and gauge, especially for new entrants to the model railway hobby?

Firstly, the challenge is to decide upon exactly what is wanted. If it's a model railway suitable for the modern restricted table top, that can subsequently be expanded and detailed, then TT:120 could be ideal. The scale supports great detail and is clearly a sensible entry-level scale for adults, however it does lack the robust 'play' element of a child's first train set, along the lines of the Hornby 'Smokey Joe' type in OO scale. As a result, TT:120 gets a similar reaction from Club members to existing N gauge (2mm scale) sets and layouts.

If you are keen on modelling a specific prototype that is not supplied 'out the box', then the restricted range in TT:120 will prove a major challenge. If you're happy to accept that you will be modelling steam or diesel based in a period and locale dictated by what has so far been produced, or indeed just want to run trains regardless, then TT:120 is worthy of serious thought.

Next come your layout ideas, and the level of detail desired. You can just about fit O gauge into less than a metre length (see *Templegate Wagon Works*, see page 16) or a complex N gauge circuit onto the size of a domestic door. You can have a OO terminus to fiddle yard in a similar size. Yet TT:120 lends itself to playability combined with the option of onward expansion. It has a degree of strength and detail above N, plus is kinder to the eyes, and less fiddly in the hand. O gauge is a great scale to super-detail in, although you need lots of space, and it's expensive to 'go large'.

Horncastle by 'Bespoke Model Building' is an example of a Lincolnshire prototype in OO. An 18ft length is required to give a spacious end-to-end layout. Reduce this by a third for TT:120.

If one is to make a specific prototype, then custom buildings are required in any case. It is just a matter of adjusting the scale of brick papers and accessories, many of which are rapidly appearing on the market thanks to the adoption of new technology by suppliers.

The full length of *Horncastle*: a nice, uncrowded layout, giving operational interest combined with a prototype target date. The downside is that it occupies a lot of space, especially in a domestic or shed setting.

Going below TT:120 to N gauge with *Manton Junction*. Yes, you can fit a lot in! There is a much wider selection of stock available than in TT, and it's the same for accessories. Wheels and flanges appear a tad out of scale when looking very closely, as does the motion on steam locomotives. TT:120 can come into its own with the degree of detail that exists in the models.

Stepping up to O gauge with *Templegate Wagon Works* by Dave Tailby. A quart into a pint pot by clever use of a sector plate (controlled by a window latch), and an overrun out the other side for shunting. Interest is maintained by changing stock and using a dice to randomise the manoeuvres being undertaken.

Comparing Scale, Ratio and Gauge

One of the challenges at the Club was the visualisation of the differences between TT:120 and the existing alternatives that were already part of members' mental maps.

For example, in TT:120 it is possible to get away with using a large N scale tree or a small one from HO/OO. If positioned correctly and of a decent 'granularity' of detail it will work. However, where buildings and accessories are concerned, it becomes much more difficult.

We recently looked at a Roco HO scale coal yard and crane, with the thought that it could be part of a coal mine disposal yard in TT:120. It appeared smaller to the OO-trained eye, and offered up to some 'soft' scenery it worked with trees and shrubs. However, once compared to our TT:120 Class 08 shunter, which is often wheeled out as a unit of measure, a sharp intake of breath and

Demonstrating the major jump between O gauge and TT:120 using the ubiquitous Class 08 'Gronk' shunter. O gauge approximates to a ratio of 1:43 – far greater than 1:120. The actual rail gap gauge here is 12mm for TT:120 and 32mm for O. Where things differ is between the portrayal of the actual track width and the rolling stock size. TT:120 is sold as the scale with a true ratio between the standard rail gauge in real life and the rolling stock placed upon it, and therefore not one that carries a historical burden where compromises need to be made. Also, while you would imagine the O gauge locomotive to be of a cost proportionately more than the TT:120 example, DCC chips and sound cubes are of a similar cost. The cost of the actual item of rolling stock is not even a multiple of two, despite the feeling of getting quite a block of material when handling the O example. We come down to aspects such as economies of scale, origination costs and detailing extras entering the frame.

rewind occurred. Thus it is always worth taking a well packed item of rolling stock with you when hunting at an exhibition so that such value judgements can be made. An unlabelled approximately 3mm-scale resin church was selected because it 'worked' with the rolling stock acid test. Some things *will* work in such 'transitions': a tall signal post for N becomes a medium one from TT:120; a favourite industrial building in N becomes a backstop perspective piece against the backscene in TT. Some components for buildings and structures from HO/OO will rescale as well – for example, Dapol/Airfix girder bridge parts can be repurposed for a wagon coal drop.

The good thing is that once the feel for TT:120 is gained by the modeller, the ability to 'borrow' from the other scales for all but track and rolling stock becomes a fun hunt, and yet another reason for taking on TT:120 before it becomes a 'mature' scale.

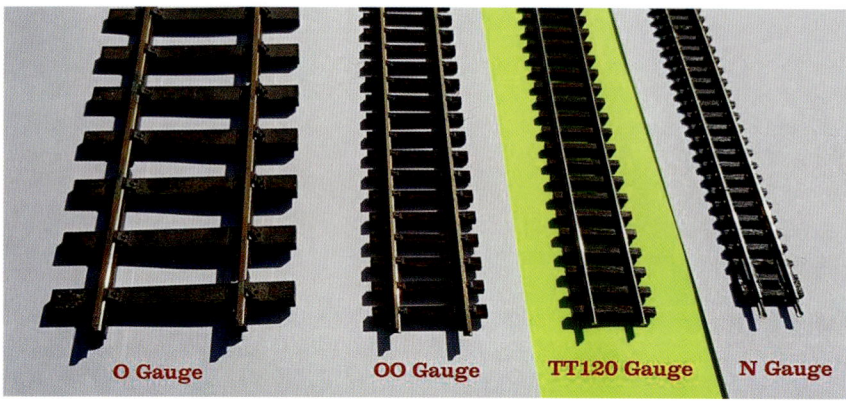

A quick comparison of ready-to-run (RTR) trackwork shows the intermediate nature of TT:120 at the smaller end of the hobby's size range between OO and N.

Left: Getting the feel of TT:120 among multiple items: the Hornby TT:120 12-ton Fisons sulphuric acid tank wagon (TT6010); an Austin low loader taxi from Oxford Diecast (120A001) and plastic injection figures from Noch. These are all designed to be true to scale. Compare a figure to doorways and windows, a vehicle to a pavement, road width or lamp posts, a wagon to lineside accessories. As a result of such comparison, the blend of items chosen need not come from a pure TT:120 range. They have to coexist, but with depth of scene, green breaks and other tricks to the eye, other scales can be successfully blended in.

Left: If a company is kind enough to make items for another scale, but you can use them, by all means indulge. A townscape with lineside allotments is about to benefit from these N gauge extras from TP Models. Everything approaches a 2m scale height in TT:120 so is good to use.

The Available Range

Hornby TT:120 products reached the market in late 2022 and were proof that you cannot provide everything for everyone all at once, especially when you have mature alternative scales to produce and compete with. This reflected the situation in 1938 when the then innovative die-cast and tinplate Hornby Dublo was released (see Chapter 11).

The initial TT:120 phase picked on some iconic locomotives such as the LNER/BR A3 and A4 express steam engines plus an 08 diesel shunter. Subsequent catalogued releases showcased what was described by some as an eclectic mix of types and eras, serving to seed the future market. They included an HST in two useful 1980s liveries, which gave us the idea to produce a Club TT:120 layout set in south-western England during that decade.

'The Easterner' boxed set (TT1002M) illustrated here was an early product review model, provided to the Club by *BRM* magazine. As such we had a few rough edges to deal with when testing. Nothing was new or insurmountable when compared to the Club team working on, for example, an old EM gauge locomotive needing renovation.

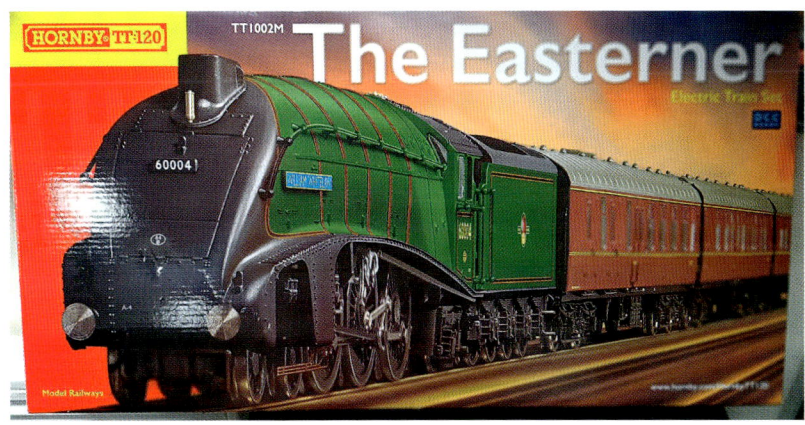

The early Hornby TT:120 train sets were analogue DC, including a locomotive with a three-pole motor and flywheel, upgradable to DCC with sound through a Next-18 interface. Later sets had this as a pre-fitted option.

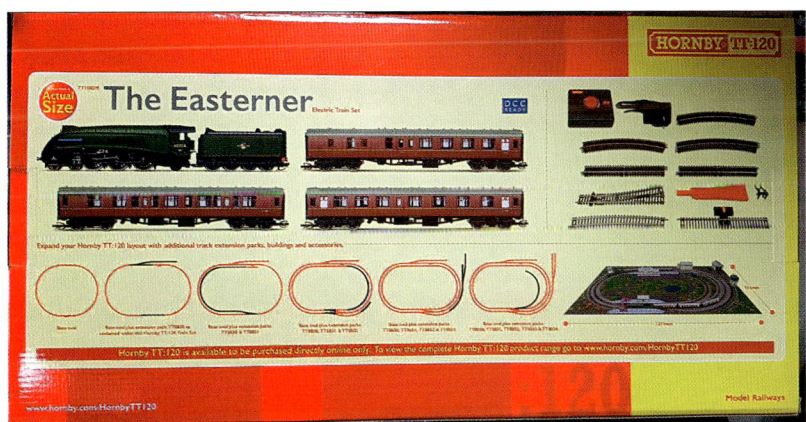

Contents of TT1002M: Class A4 steam locomotive; 3 x Mark 1 passenger coaches; oval of track (track pack 1); re-railer tool; analogue controller.

The overall track length is 2,940mm, with a track footprint of 1,370mm x 910mm, which equates to a modern tabletop. The adoption of NEM couplings aids the rolling stock's ability to tackle tight radius curves.

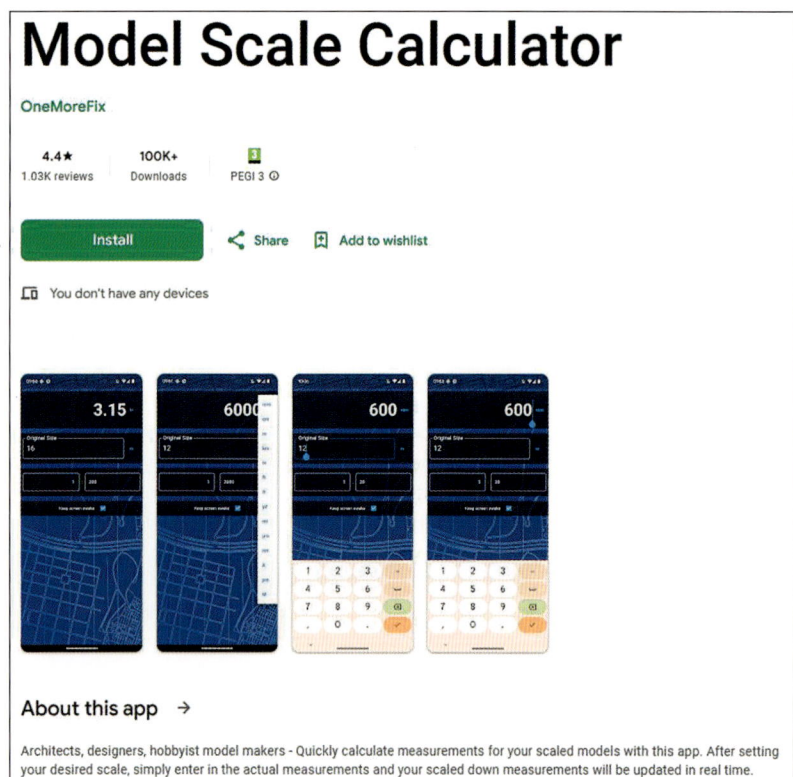

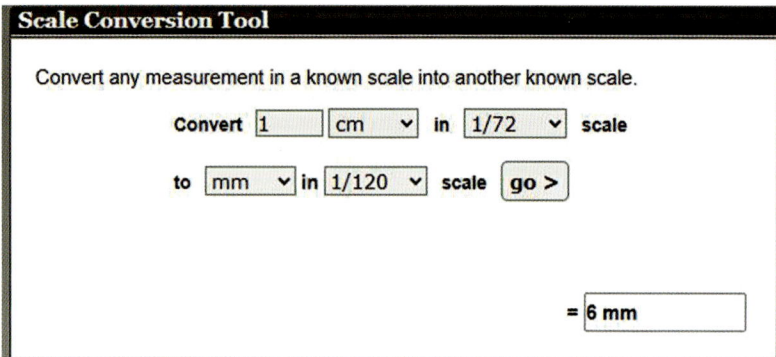

Left and middle: Playing the scales game can make the head spin. There is a useful Model Scale Calculator available from Google Play or the Apple Store. Alternatively, try that provided by https://www.scalemodelersworld.com/online-scale-converter-tool.html#aScaleConvert. If resizing a 3D or paper print from OO, the true adjustment ratio is: OO 100% = TT:120 63.35%.

Below: The initial release of the A3/A4 locomotive by Hornby proved to seasoned modellers that the scale was capable of high detail plus chip control and sound from the start. Small but frustrating issues such as the front steps on the A3 fouling the bogie on tighter curves, and some mechanical failures, needed sorting. Early adoption in any industry has problems, but hobbyists take it personally!

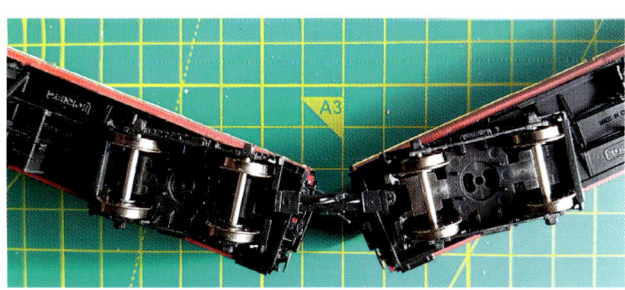

To sell the concept of TT:120 to Club members and the coordinating committee we concentrated on the carriage rolling stock. The amount of detail present on such a small item can get lost to the older eye unless blown up and projected. Not as fiddly as N, the compactness of TT:120 in comparison to OO makes items feel more 'engineered'.

By the time the Class 50 came onto the shelves we had a working proposition for our first TT:120 layout. Here is DCC chip and sound 50 007 *Sir Edward Elgar* (ex-*Hercules*) re-liveried for GWR 150 celebrations in 1985, which on the Club layout would pull Mark 1 carriage specials along the Devon seafront, alternating with an A4.

3
The Club Challenge – *Holcombe Beach*

Paddington Station, 07:45 on 3 April 1980 at the start of the Easter holiday rush. On platform 2, unit 253024 will tail the train whisking the author's family to the West Country. By now the railways were on the back foot. No longer the steam-days' crush, when a train would have several relief services at time intervals after the departure of the primary express. When Hornby announced the timely release of two livery variants of HST units, the Devon coast became a viable primary project focus for the Club's TT:120 layout.

The MDMRC Essendine Club room on 23 February 2023: Howard Smith of *BRM* magazine goes through the project proposals with club seniors. At this point we had no demo samples of TT:120, just some printed publicity information. Some members privately joined the Hornby TT:120 Club to get a feel for the product. It was a beginning, but certainly not of a type we were used to – no track, no stock – but with a fixed date for completion.

Some starts are more memorable than others. First step: we had no track or rolling stock to get the feel of the new scale. Hidden away in the Club room there was some continental flexitrack which approximated to TT:120 for testing curvature, and eBay came to the rescue with some curve guides in Perspex. Combine these assets with some donated scrap board (which was previously a tombstone in a theatrical production) and you end up with an interesting yet perhaps rather foreboding project launch experience.

The first build-up team convenes in the Club workspace inside the test track. Innovation was the name of the game: new scale, new board technique, new Bluetooth DCC; challenges all over. Ideas mooted were built upon, rejected, resurrected, executed, then reworked as problems were encountered. Our train set and first grasp of the product arrived in April 2023. The team of fifteen (with a combined age approaching 1,000 years) unboxed it like kids at a childhood Christmas. Initial thoughts were that the finished product was of a high quality, somewhat 'dinky' in scale (especially for those used to O or OO), and it was fiddly to put the track together. Interestingly, the Hornby set-track curved rails were found to not lie flat, and were slightly more than a full circle. However, if pinned down on a board this was not seen as a problem.

Far left and left: Once track was purchased we discovered that mix and match between Hornby and Peco was not an exact science. The gauge was good – the track face section, however, differed. We could either buy an expensive conversion section, do some gentle filing or, in our case, use OO joiners and then cut them in half with a rotary cutting disc.

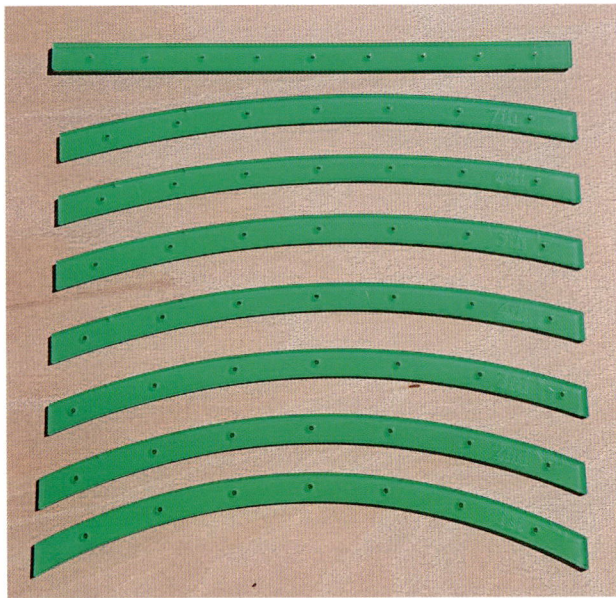

Having a set of curve guides for gauge and scale is a wise move when using flexitrack. Here the set goes from straight, through seventh radius down to a tight first-radius curve. If there are any rolling stock restrictions they get published. For the initial offerings in TT:120 the rolling stock articulation is very good, allowing for tight curves to be utilised if required.

As mentioned previously, early in 2023 the club was approached by BRM magazine with a proposition to construct a display layout in TT:120 scale. It had to be within the skills reach of the 'average' person, make use of innovative materials and techniques, and be completed and available from February 2024 for the annual display circuit.

Although individual members had looked at the prospect of dabbling with TT:120, it had never crossed our minds as a Club, since it was still new to the market and with a limited portfolio of rolling stock and accessories.

There was a good legacy of cooperation. We had worked with BRM previously on our OO Amberdale and Canons Cross layouts. They were intended to show what could be fitted into a small garden shed using easy constructional techniques. Both later appeared on the national display circuit after being expanded in size and complexity, and they still serve us well over ten years later. They were mothballed when the show vandalism took place in spring 2019, and then came out of retirement to face the front line again.

Many of the crew responsible for constructing Amberdale now formed the experienced core of the team building a south-western coastal scene in TT:120, provisionally titled The Devon Riviera, set in the late 1980s and focused on the Teignmouth area.

There were a number of questions at the back of our minds, primary among which was whether TT:120 would have enough rolling stock diversity to produce a layout that would maintain interest. It seemed that the purchase of boxed sets would be the norm, with less interest from Hornby in expanding the overall locomotive or rolling stock range at that time.

People seem to think of rail on the south Devon coastline in two contradictory ways: the sunny, calm holiday image with steam or later travel, with crowds of happy holidaymakers watching a train go by, or the of a challenging, albeit visually impressive, storm-lashed line where rolling stock gets a thorough salt bath. Very much man verses nature. Here, heading west towards Dawlish station, is a First Great Western HST set, on a tranquil 22 July 2018. (David Dixon CC BY-SA 2.0 Geograph contribution)

Cliff Without the Shadows: a practice diorama based on American HO scale was the ideal testbed for the techniques to be used. Built by Alan Hancock, this polystyrene hillscape had a plaster top covering using commercial rubber or home-made kitchen foil moulds, blended together with Sculptamold. It showed that we could use impressive cliffs without overshadowing the railway element. (*Alan Hancock*)

Geology

I must observe that no man can be more sensible than I am of the great advantage it would be to me as a civil engineer to be better acquainted with geology, as well as with many other branches of science.

Isambard Kingdom Brunel

Given that our Devon coast model would include open cliff exposures that are known to so many, it was determined that we had to study the geology in more depth than would normally occur in building a model railway. The variations in steepness, overgrowth and strata faulting needed to be understood, so that we could correctly represent them. A couple of geography graduates in the team made good use of the published British Geological Society memoirs, and of a wonderful website by Dr Ian West (ex-Southampton University, https://wessexcoastgeology.soton.ac.uk).

The cliff exposures along the railway frontage from Dawlish Warren in the east to Teignmouth in the west are Palaeozoic formations. Impressive in both form and colouration, they represent the last period of the Palaeozoic, the Permian, some 299 to 252 million years ago.

The earlier Devonian or later Triassic periods often steal the limelight in the common mind, especially when thought is given to Devon's red soils and rocks. These Permian exposures are a deep purple, red-hued, iron-rich, and capture a feel of extreme arid conditions, open deserts, wadi formations and shifting sand dunes.

The subtle changes in rock type on the Dawlish to Teignmouth stretch bring differing challenges to the railway builder (both Brunel and Market Deeping), with headlands, tunnels, landslips and sea exposure to the predominant south-westerly winds.

Sprey Point, for example, is a consolidated landslip. Inadvertently the slip was stabilised due to the weight of the 'toe' of material being consolidated by the retaining walls at the foot of the cliff. There are still rockfalls, mainly triggered by subsoil water, and the path and eventually the clifftop houses will be threatened, as will train services.

If you walk along the sea wall from Teignmouth to Holcombe, with the cliffs towering to your left, you will see stable

Ex-GWR 4-6-0 Hall class 5992 *Horton Hall* speeds elegantly past holidaymakers with the down 'Cornishman' summer relief. This is prior to any remedial landslip works on the cliff face near Sprey Point. Research supposes that some of the semaphore signals were linked to wires that would bring trains to a stand in the event of a rockfall. (*Ben Brookbank Geograph CC BY-SA 2.0 Deed*)

Permian breccia cliffs (angular shattered rock fragments in a fine matrix) which have a steep incline and overgrowth. Halfway to Sprey Point these breccia cliffs were artificially sloped in the 1920s since steam train burn-outs of foliage led to cliff falls after heavy rain. Beyond the historic slip at Sprey Point the rock face continues as breccia with a number of vertical fracture lines weakening it.

At the headland of Parsons Tunnel the rock type is similar to elsewhere but of a redder colour. There are larger boulders in the desert outwash wadis and less fracturing by natural fracking (water trapped when the deposits were laid down fractured the strata when under pressure). The Smugglers Lane valley represents a fault line between rocks of different sea resistance. The face of the fault is where the tunnel enters.

Physical and Human Geography

The cliffs have a fairly consistent height and colour, with Parsons Tunnel and the headland sticking out to sea as major identifiable features. Modelling these in detail helps to anchor the right side of the layout and hide the return curve of track to the fiddle yard.

Verdant growth of the South African hottentot fig (a Cape region invader of southern England) occupies much of the sand faces of the cliffs. After the age of steam, when much of the growth was either cut back or accidentally burned back, the cliff faces became hidden by fig and other accompanying sand-tolerating species. The target date of our railway model represents a mid-point of foliage coverage, away from landslip points which show as clean rock.

The sea wall protecting both cliff and railway has reduced the material reaching the beach, so at times just a rocky platform shows. This allows full-force waves to hit the sea wall – an ideal location to show wave activity in alternate calm and rough sea scenes in model form.

Sprey Point was the natural choice for the mid-section, since it then hides the front baseboard join. The tunnel mouth and headland hide the other.

The urban sprawl of Teignmouth as a seaside town in the 1980s would be shown on the painted model backscene, but not the model itself. It aided our build schedule to keep the coastal fringe as distant woodland, because not many model buildings existed in TT:120 at that early stage. Similar thinking was applied with regards to Holcombe to the right-hand side of the layout, with just the hotel on the clifftop and Smugglers Lane representing the route to the village itself.

We were extremely fortunate in the varied photography existing for this part of the coast railway. Here at 07:40 on a cloudless Wednesday 9 April 1975 the 05:05 from Penzance to Paddington speeds through behind a very clean Class 52 Western diesel. Approaching withdrawal, many Westerns were looking dull and unkempt from the chemical washers, and a lamentable lack of attention. By February 1977 all Westerns had retired from service. (*Roger Geach Geograph CC BY-SA 2.0 Deed*)

Historical Research

Cornwall is such that no railway can be constructed at moderate expense without either sacrificing all consideration for the interest of localities and the position of the population to the mere choice of levels, or without steep gradients and sharp curves.

Isambard Kingdom Brunel

Much the same could be said of his treatment of Devon, cutting cliff and beach off from the populace.

One of benefits of being in a model railway club is the mixed backgrounds and interests of the members. Keen amateur historians, geographers and geologists are scattered

The Starcross atmospheric pumping station in 2022. A remarkable survivor of the early railway, albeit with a shortened tower today. The aim was for a stationary engine to create a vacuum in a cast pipe, forcing the 'pig' attached to a carriage to move. These pipes had an upper surface slot with a greased leather seal to maintain the negative pressure. An unforeseen side effect was that mice and rats were attracted to eat the leather and tallow animal grease. Apart from loss of vacuum pressure, a number of dead rodents also arrived at the pumping stations at speed on startup.

An image taken of an atmospheric railway model in the Newton Abbot Museum. Had Brunel's idea worked, the railway would have lacked the active atmosphere that has drawn enthusiasts and modellers. As it was, the scheme was underpowered, plus expensive to run and repair.

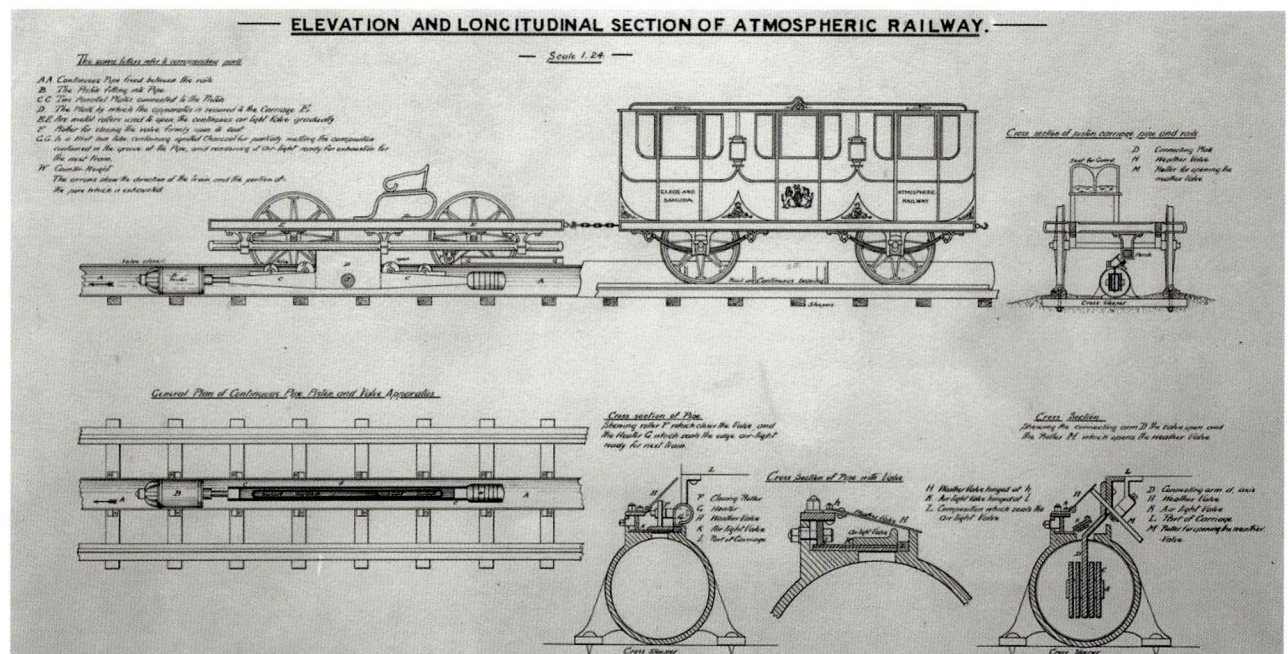

Jacob and Joseph Samuda of the Southwark ironworks in London along with Samuel Clegg developed an 1835 atmospheric system for two years of testing at Wormwood Scrubs. By 1846, five miles of the Croydon Railway was laid with pipework. Brunel visited and experimented there, and at an Irish scheme in Dalkey. (*Colombia University*)

within our ranks. The Dawlish to Teignmouth coastline triggered the grey cells of many members, spawning site visits, photography and a desire to get things correct and in context.

The requirement for a level route to the south-west of England dates back to a grand experiment by the venerable I.K. Brunel and his ill fated atmospheric railway scheme. The original railway plans were to place the line further out to sea, since a wave-cut platform of solid rocks underpins this part of the coast for a distance offshore. It would have been completely level, but far more open to storms.

This weather factor soon disabused planners of that course of action. The 'Great Gale' or 'Great Storm' (thought to be a possible hurricane) of 22–23 November 1824 with a 3–4m above mean high-tide surge had caused extensive damage and deaths along the south coast. Dawlish Warren, Sidmouth, Lyme Regis Cobb, Chesil Beach and Hurst Castle Spit all suffered. In Weymouth, there is a memorial stone for the esplanade destroyed by the tempest. This gale would have been fresh in local memory when the civil engineering visitors first came down to Dawlish and Teignmouth via the London stagecoach.

The first heavy sea experiment of a sea-wall splash. How can one create a maelstrom on a model railway? Answer – a mixture of resin with fibreglass car filler, clear modelling resin and acrylic paint, with some further refinement of colour, and peaks and troughs to create the required wave sequence. The aim was to portray a scene of violent attack on the last trains able to run that day, just before coastal rail services were suspended.

The Day Chosen

Since we were portraying rolling stock liveries of the late 1980s, a specific date for our rough seas came to the fore. The day building up to the Great Storm of 1987 was chosen: Thursday 15 October. This is the day when, infamously, weatherman Michael Fish commented to a Welsh TV viewer that there was no hurricane coming. Technically correct – it was a very deep depression with a sting jet in the tail, accelerating the wind speed.

As well as increasing variability and interest in what in effect was to be a simple looped layout, the date chosen allowed for an extra dimension at exhibitions by swapping out seaside display cartridges. We could thus alternate between a normal low-tide beach and an impressive stormy high tide washing over the sea wall. Our display information boards could also contain deeper factual details to bring the scene to life.

Due to a combination of trees down over railway lines and extensive power outages, the railway system was severely dislocated on Friday 16 October 1987. Seen here is the sign in the window of Honor Oak Station, SE London. (*David Wright CC BY-SA 2.0*)

During this weather event, sustained winds of 86mph (139km/h) with accompanying gusts of 134mph (216km/h) were experienced in the English Channel. Today this would be termed by journalists as a 'weather bomb'.

During the day of the 15th a depression moved north-east from the Bay of Biscay, deepening as it reached the shores of Cornwall and Brittany. The area around Dawlish and Teignmouth did not receive the strongest winds, although neighbouring Dorset caught a nasty sideswipe with extensive damage as the winds hit storm force 11 and the pressure dropped to 953mb. The *Daily Mail* reported of a geography field trip of children on Chesil Beach, Dorset, where at 5pm they were constantly being blown over as the waves got bigger. To the west, a huge, dark bank of cloud had appeared. At the same time the temperature rose by 8°C in under half an hour. The core of the storm tracked over Prawle Point in south Devon at 1.30 am the next morning.

Overall this storm took twenty-two lives and at 1987 prices a damage cost was estimated at £12bn. It is listed in the Met Office day book for 16 October simply as the 'Great Storm'.

It is an event lodged in memory, and as far as we know a railway model has not been tied to it. The weather forecasting community was much shaken by it. To quote the BBC's Michael Buerk when grilling weatherman Ian McCaskill the next morning: 'Well, Ian, you chaps were a fat lot of good last night! If you can't forecast the worst storms for several centuries three hours before they happen, what are you doing?'

```
TELEX ****    ****    ****    ****    ****
MORNING FORECAST
SEA AREA PORTLAND

GALE WARNING
    Issued on behalf of the Meteorological
    Office: 08:52 (UTC) on Thu 15 Oct 1987

    Southwesterly gale force 8 expected later,
    increasing severe gale force 9 later backing
    southerly
WIND
    Westerly or southwesterly 4 to 6.
SEA STATE
    Rough or very rough, becoming very rough or high
    seas later.
WEATHER
    Rain or squally showers.
VISIBILITY
    Good, occasionally poor.


TELEX ****    ****    ****    ****    ****
LATE FORECAST (ADJUSTED URGENT)
SEA AREA PORTLAND

ATTENTION ALL SHIPPING GALE WARNING
    Issued on behalf of the Meteorological
    Office: 01:40 (UTC) on Fri 16 Oct 1987

    Imminent Southwesterly Storm force 10
    occasionally veering Southerly Violent storm
    force 11
WIND
    Southwesterly or southerly gale 8 -9.
SEA STATE
    High or very High seas imminent.
WEATHER
    Persistent Rain or squally showers.
VISIBILITY
    Poor or very poor.
```

As a club that actively displays model railways at shows, we like to give a backstory through information boards. It helps viewers understand the portrayal by giving some depth, and occasionally drama, to the viewing experience. One thing we could not locate was a full gale warning in the public domain. So we back-engineered a telex printout covering the build-up to the storm by drawing definitions from the Met Office marine forecasts glossary, combined with weather chart facts published from the days in question. Even if you have a home-only layout, this sort of extra tangential information is great for visitors, and also helps keep the layout build mission on target. Interestingly, although it sits in common memory as a 'hurricane', including tornadoes and high sustained winds, the Great Storm was never forecast as such, even to maritime recipients or emergency services. 'Violent storm 11 with 56–63 knots wind' was as high as it got, even when weather stations reported greater velocity. At the time, pressure and observation charts were at least an hour behind, being drawn by hand, with much weather station and ship data coming in later. Shoreham-by-Sea in Sussex reported 100 knots (120mph, 190km/h) before failure of the anemometer. There is a wonderful quotation from *The Times* of 17 October 1987: 'Peacetime Echo of the Blitz'. When future generations crowd at the knee to ask: 'What did you do in the Great Wind, Daddy?' the boldest will answer for sure, 'I walked'.

The Baseboard

One of the requirements of the layout was to make use of innovative, lightweight materials. The main substrate was to be insulation blocks such as those produced by Kingspan or Celotex. While not the cheapest of options, they are lightweight, durable, resist sagging and theoretically would not vary with the heat and humidity changes experienced at an exhibition.

Downsides were also to be found with this material – the edges needed protection, it would not take simple glue and nails for trackwork and cutting it brought forth excessive dust.

For home use, in theory a tabletop-size single sheet without any extra aids could be used. The edges could then be painted or taped to prevent damage. For exhibition use, however, we had to properly protect the edges, incorporate board joints with location pins, and allow for car transportation. As a result we developed a lightweight framing for the baseboard, allowing it to go on top of trestle legs. Usefully, this framing means that the flat fiddle yard boards can be inverted to protect the main front scenic boards in transit, by bolting spacing end boards into place.

At the Club we make models. It's both useful and fun sometimes to make a scale 'pre-model' of your concept to put plans into context. We borrowed the incomplete baseboard of our OO *Mitchell Junction* layout, and put the five insulation boards into their set resting places. Then we set up the mock-up model to discuss the finer points of support, framing and line positioning. As TT:120 was new to all of us, the challenge here was not running out of space while retaining decent curve geometry.

A plan was drawn up using 'AnyRail' software, but somehow we ended up with good old fashioned manual drawing on a template representing the boards. In many ways it was refreshing to get back to basics and overcome any technical challenges based on long experience.

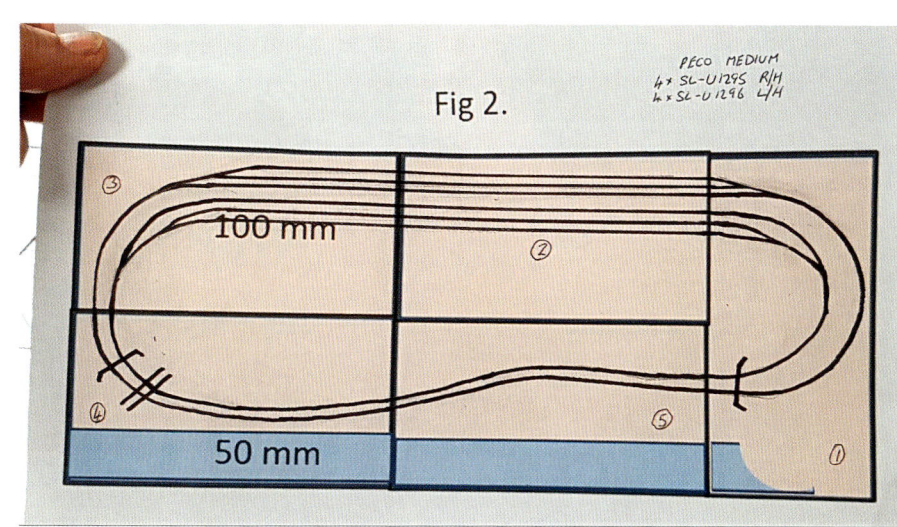

A lightweight ply external frame was braced in the corners and given a rim against which the insulation blocks could be glued. The desire was to have a lightweight and temperature-stable surface for the running lines and scenery. In actuality, a skin of thin plywood was required along with some sunken and glued wood blocks to allow joins and trackbed to be secure.

Another challenge: how to carry the boards to shows? Rudimentary racking was constructed to go into a box trailer. Individual boards slotted in, like a chest of drawers. Cable ties were used to secure the inserts and prevent them wandering around in transit.

Much thought was given to the trackbed of the coastal railway. Presented directly to the viewer it had to look right. Close cooperation with Maxey Models and Ballast led to a fine blend of real aggregates taken from the actual quarries supplying Network Rail (far left). At times, you just cannot beat the real thing.

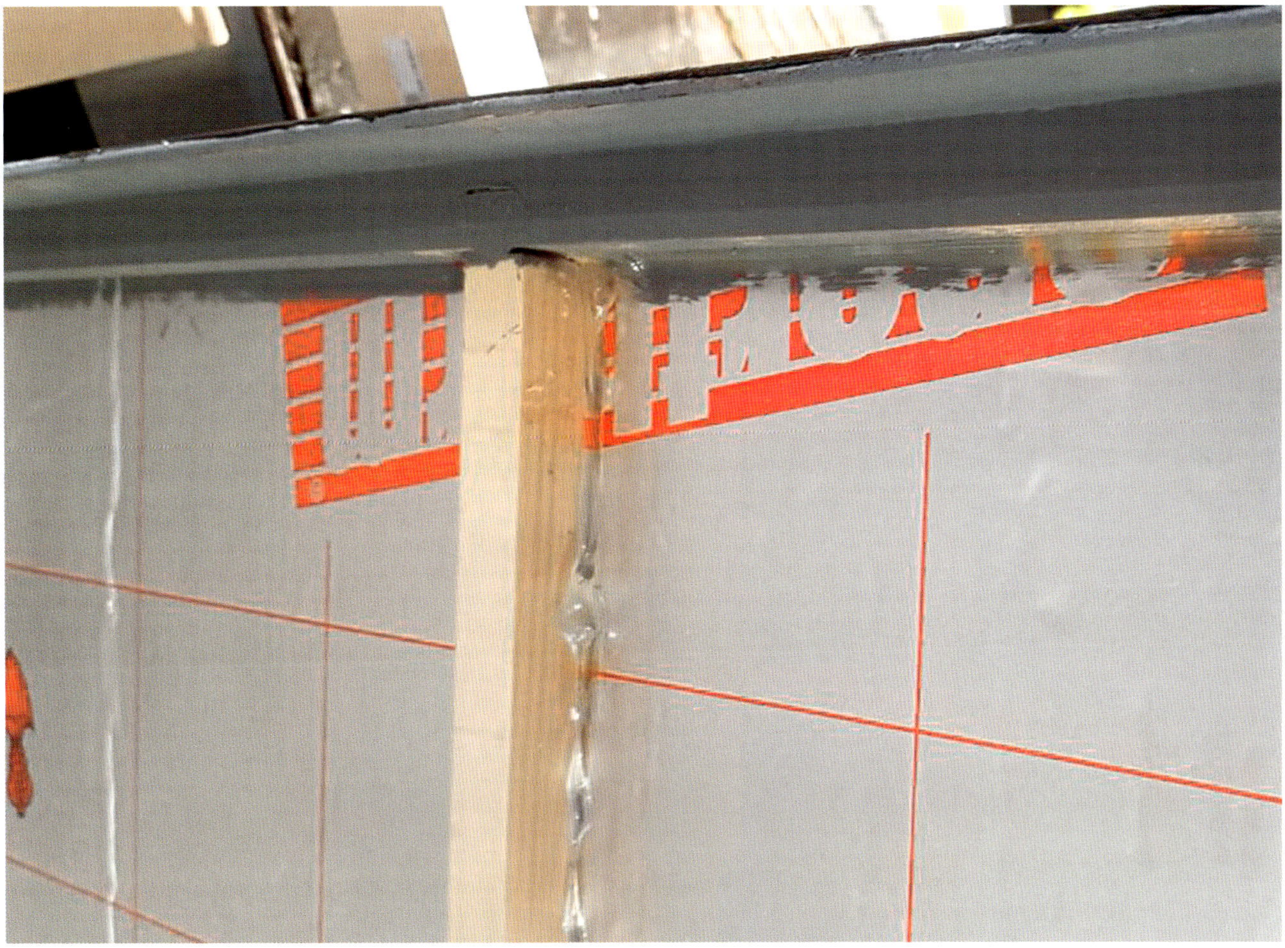

The underside of a board, showing the dovetailed joint for a cross support. While this could be screwed or plated, traditional methods are quite valid as well. Clear domestic kitchen silicon sealant was used to retain frame and board, since it has some 'give' to it, allowing for movement of the different materials.

This is where the mock-up model from the planning stage and the finished item are comparable. Above all else, the mock-up ensured that there were no bad surprises for the team with the finished product. What one cannot see is how cold it was at setup. All components had shrunk beyond expectation, apart from the boards themselves.

Above, left and below: The completed baseboards seen here being set up at the BRM Doncaster show, February 2024. Despite careful planning, joining bolts between the boards were thin on the ground, leading us to hurriedly purchase replacements. In this location the external frame catches came into their own. They are adjustable, which is ideal since the lighter weight wood framing needs different levels of tightness, as heat and humidity vary swiftly during a show day. A home-built layout with this base material would be far more stable.

Occasionally a product is released just in time. In this case rakes of BP, ESSO, and Total TTA 45-ton tankers. The underside detailing at this scale was regarded by the team as superb. The 08 easily pulls ten wagons along the Devon coast.

Although the 1980s is ancient history to some in the hobby, to many it is seemingly yesterday. We wanted to evoke the archetypal childhood summer holiday. The heart goes back to a simpler time when a camping coach with basic facilities at the seaside or country station was enough for a family holiday.

Seen here is ex-GWR clerestory camping coach W9905W at Falmouth station on 22 June 1962. (*Online Transport Archive—Meredith 500-6*)

4
The Seafront

Telephoto view from Dawlish station past the sea wall at Coryton Cove, over to the rear of Parsons Tunnel at Holcombe. The rock stack of the Parson can be seen, although maps through time have interchanged the position of Parson, Clerk and Shag Rock, leaving things quite confused. Here in 2023 there is extensive remedial work being undertaken to prevent rockfall, including the building of a substantial avalanche shelter.

The early sea wall was prone to substantial damage by extreme weather, as demonstrated here in a sketch by F.W.L. Stockdale from 1855. The event here occurred on 12 February at Parson and Clerk when parts of the sea wall were damaged, and a 70yd (64m) section was washed away to be replaced by a temporary viaduct. The isolated stack is probably Shag Rock, which lost much of its height in a storm during 1984, and was then effectively beheaded in January 2003. (Illustrated London News, *3 March 1855*)

The South Devon Railway sea wall was damaged and blocked many times over the years. The table shows the extent of the major problems suffered. Even in 2023, despite extensive rebuilding in the Dawlish area, there was still damage being sustained elsewhere, to the extent of the Smugglers Lane Viaduct and sea wall both receiving material damage in that year's autumn 'named' storms.

Year	Days blocked	Reason	Locale
1846	3	Wall damage	Breeches Rock
1852	7	Rockfall	Breeches Rock
1853	4	Rockfall	Kennaway Tunnel
1855	12	Wall damage	Smugglers Lane
1859	3	Wall damage	Teignmouth
1872	1	Wall damage	Langstone
1873	3	Wall damage	Langstone
1923	3	Rockfall	Sprey Point
1930	5	Wall damage	Dawlish Riviera Terrace
1936	12	Wall damage	Powderham
1986	6	Wall damage	Sprey Point
2006	1	Wall damage	Dawlish Rockstone
2014	28	Wall damage	Dawlish Riviera Terrace
2014	28	Rockfall	Holcombe

One of the GWR's twenty allocated DMU units of Class 150/2. Here Sprinter 207 is heading from Dawlish to Teignmouth in sparkling early summer weather on 26 June 2023. Passing under Lea Mount via the Kennaway Tunnel, it will then emerge in Coryton Cove. The tunnel entrance was blocked by a fall in 1853, and the interesting recurved arch shows the response to such instability of the cliff.

Network Rail and local council operatives working on the Kennaway Tunnel cliffs to the Dawlish side, due to the footpath having sustained a rockfall.

The general seafront being modelled has Sprey Point positioned at the break of a baseboard. This is an annotated 1889 6in map of the coastal railway. When researching, online mapping resources such as the National Library of Scotland historical OS maps, as well as aerial satellite shots from Google Earth and others are invaluable. (*Reproduced with the permission of the National Library of Scotland*)

Sandy Bay in N, by Kevin and Maggie Smith. This features a gentle sea and the recurve of beach up to a retaining groyne. Longshore drift of beach materials is right to left, the opposite of its action on the Club layout.

On *Sandy Bay*, the bay area takes the water deeper into the layout. The task with Smugglers Lane Viaduct on the far east of board 2 of the Club layout was to give the small three-arch viaduct and inlet a sense of depth.

Dunstan Harbour, Northumberland, in 4mm by Alan Blackburn and Norman Cook is the opposite extreme. The sea is active, with waves lapping aggressively up against the mole in mid-harbour.

At the rear of *Dunstan Harbour* the waves are nearly topping the sea wall. The chaos of the refracted waves is well represented by the opaque finish of the Modroc. Unlike a smooth sea, no real transparency or reflection is required.

Mini Project: A Seaside Test

If you have doubts about your skill set when attempting some feature on a layout, try taking it off into a mini diorama and learn without having to demolish a bad result. Sometimes a good result can be incorporated into the main board. This is what we did with the beach scene for the Devon layout.

Basic construction materials gathered: some 5mm plywood, sandpaper, foamboard, a pebble from Dawlish beach to act as a rock and a 3D print of a sea wall.

Lego is great for delimiting castings, since it forms a flexibly-sized yet rigid 'curtain wall' once a plastic barrier, such as a plastic bag, has been put in place. Here we also have acrylic ultramarine blue to act as a stain to the resin and a matt white enamel for wave crests and spume.

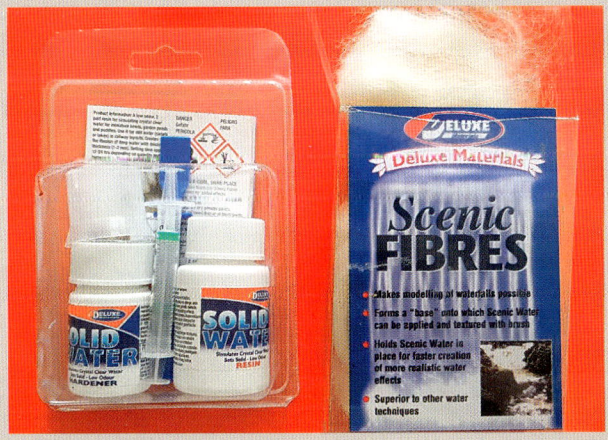

There are a number of alternatives for creating water features. In this case we aimed to produce a permanent casting with wave effects, so Deluxe Materials Solid Water and Scenic Fibres were chosen.

The foamboard was carved to represent the beach gradient and the sandpaper was overlaid as the basic beach effect. The aim was in part to limit the amount of resin being used as that is the expensive element of the project.

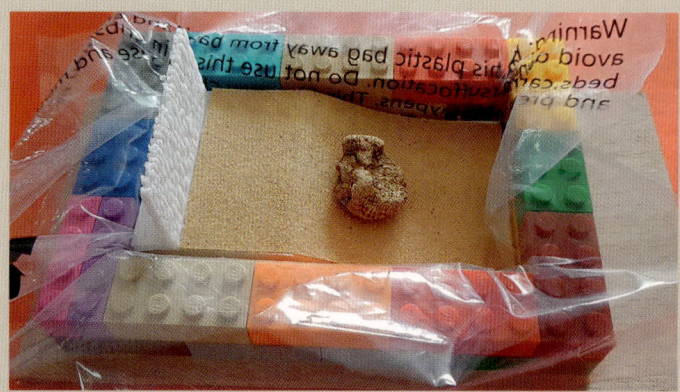

The Lego 'bund wall' is now ready and lined with an old plastic bag. The single rock for this test is glued in place. Near Teignmouth, resistant rock strata appears at lower tide due to the reduction in beach material in recent years. The plywood acts as the physical, flat casting base, but is not a part of the finished product.

Scenic fibres are brushed gently into place. They can be used in waterfalls as well to retain and guide resin. For turning waves, one plan was to use the 1cm length fibreglass that is added to cement to strengthen it.

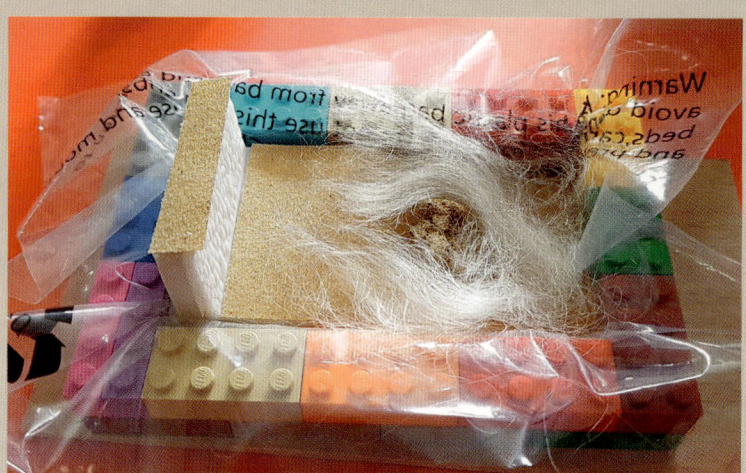

The two-part resin was mixed with a dab of blue acrylic to introduce colour. Fair weather seas reflect the sky and clouds, so this represents the light scatter on the waves. When the resin had set, we began to highlight waves and bubble zones in depth before the next pouring. The aim was to produce a degree of transparency and the illusion of trapped movement.

Finally the wall was painted and a cusp of pebbles put in place before the resin has gone off, allowing some to appear dragged into the surf. The next challenge was to scale this up without breaking the bank!

Calm Waters

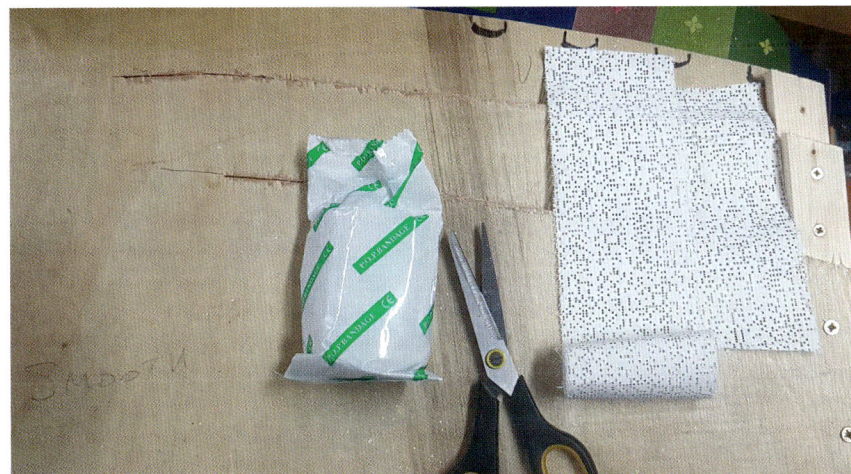

Both calm and stormy sea scenes required some special treatment for the large board for the eastern beach. To make Smugglers Lane Viaduct look realistic we had to make the valley deeper than desired, by dropping the beach below sea level! Similar actions can be required on a board where track is raised or dropped on a gradient. A number of lines were drawn and cut. Then the plywood was forced down to the spacers.

Traditional plaster bandage was used to construct a decent terrain that could then be blended into the rest of the beach.

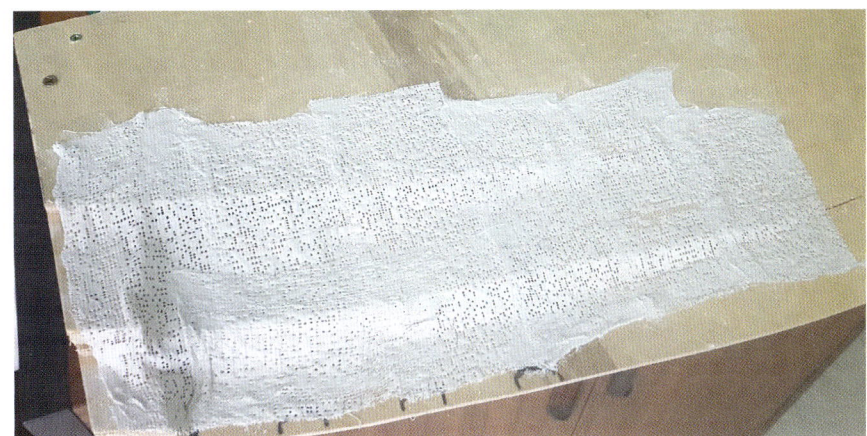

Painting with the desired beach base brown and also aquamarine for offshore as the sea increases in depth. With any scenic element, think like a fresco painter: work in different colours while the previous paint is still wet. With acrylics that have retained some 'stickiness', the blending is gentle without runs.

Aggregates can be a pain. Often they will change colour once diluted PVA has been applied. We wanted the real sand from the location to retain its look and feel. We discovered that using thick PVA with an aggregate layer poured on top would ensure there was a firm base. Then, with the PVA dry, to ensure that everything remained in situ without colour change, we used a spray adhesive.

Establishing a transparent flood fill berm (a flat strip of land) for retaining the liquid resin. In the past, attempts had been made with wood, plaster and transparent silicon, but never had finesse. This time around we used the Making Waves product from Deluxe Materials.

Deluxe Materials Solid Water was mixed to start the hardening reaction. The beach slopes gently up to deepen the fill towards the front. The berm dried transparent, providing the ideal medium for this activity. We will use this on rivers and canals in future, where such level changes or protection are needed.

Ensure the resin has hardened before moving or working with it. Drying time varies according to temperature and humidity. If ripples are needed they can be produced once a skin has formed. Be aware that sometimes they level out again and catch you out. Here the breakwater is being wet-scribed with a cocktail stick onto a PVA/plaster mix put over the foamboard former.

The endgame: the wavelets heading to shore, created using the Making Waves product. With any water feature, try to refer to images or videos to get a feel for water behaviour. The reward is the general feeling of real life in miniature without having to stretch the imagination too much. The wavelets were overpainted with white and cobalt acrylics on a nearly dry brush.

Stormy Seas

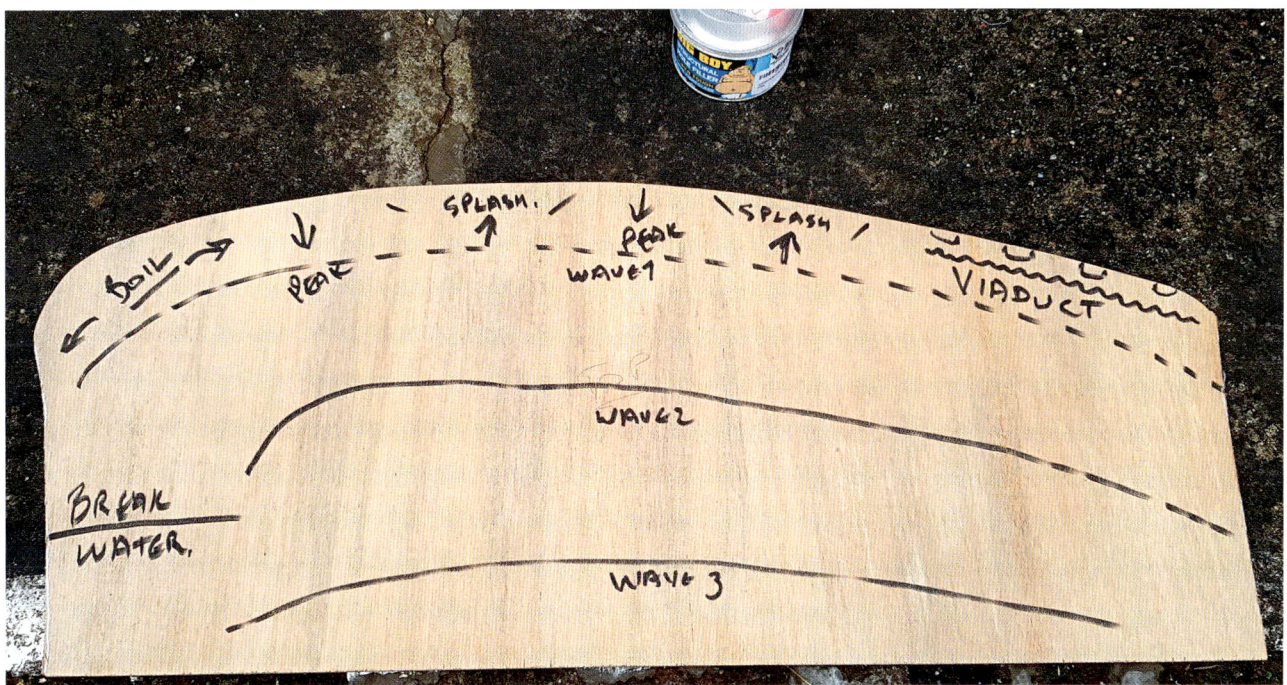

The storm board for the eastern side of the bay. The breakwater is under the surface, but is responsible for earlier wave cresting. This results in a lower energy, chaotic boiling of the water beyond, as the wave profile is broken. In line with rip currents in calmer water, there has to be an escape of the previous wave as the next hits. This is why there are sporadic wave splashes on the wall, as opposed to the whole length splashing up at the same time. So we have splashes and peak returns marked. The most complex wave forms will be near Parsons Tunnel and Smugglers Lane Viaduct due to the coastal protection blocks added here.

Car repair filler resin with fibreglass such as Isopon P40 or Big Boy hole filler was used to construct the rough waves. This is a two-part mix of a very smelly (until set) resin incorporating glass fibre, plus a hardener to mix in. Since it uses a chemical reaction to fix the resin, it was setting successfully within fifteen minutes. This was despite it being 5°C outside, working where the smell could dissipate. As 'Riviera' was intended as a display layout, it had to be able to survive shocks and knocks in transit. Less durable alternatives for the waves, such as paper and varnish, were tested but not used.

46 • DEVELOPING A MODEL RAILWAY IN TT:120 SCALE

Wavefronts were drawn out on the board based on photographs of the sea wall during stormy weather. Although no beach would be seen, in real life much lighter-weight material would be in suspension, discolouring the water.

Each successive wavefront was worked from flat board into a crest, using a plastic applicator to create peaks in the opposite manner to repairing a vehicle, where the smoothness of finish is the aim.

Closest to the sea wall is an area of turbulence. Some wave peaks crest the wall, others are suppressed by the weight of the returning rip current causing a peak against the next wave.

Getting the correct colour is key. This sea would have been accompanied by cloudy conditions, so the rich blue of the calm morning is replaced by a mid marine blue/green. A photograph was chosen and an acrylic test pot purchased at the local paint centre. Fortunately they are used to the strange pigment requests from Club members: in this case 'National Trust Aquamarine'.

What was nicknamed 'The Boil' by the modelling team is located on the eastern side of Sprey Point. Here, walls at different angles create cross-waves. As we couldn't wait around in Devon for bad weather (it behaved impeccably every time a team member visited) a chance visit to Sandown on the Isle of Wight caught just the discoloured frothing required. On the opposite facing coast from Sandown, Shanklin Pier was destroyed by the Great Storm of 1987.

The wood surface colour was allowed to bleed through, representing beach sand in suspension. Next a white acrylic was worked into position. This highlights wave crests with the drag trail giving the effect of movement. In reality the surface layers of seawater are transmitting a wave form, with particles in motion locally.

Primary detailing complete. Modellers are often deeply critical of their own work. Step away from whatever is being done, return later wIth an open mind. If you can feel movement, see detail, and almost hear the noise, then it is working well.

At Sprey Point is the Teignmouth sign, facing the railway so that passengers know where they are. This landmark needed recreation on the layout, though it has its back to the viewers. (*Richard Rogerson Geograph CC BY-SA 2.0 Deed*)

Sprey Point as seen from the west. Low scrub and shrubs replace what was a tea shop and mini golf course from earlier years. The Teignmouth sign is to the extreme right. Here on a chilly Saturday, 31 March 1979, 50 002 *Superb* passes with an express. (*Richard Rogerson Geograph CC BY-SA 2.0 Deed*)

Approaching Christmas 2023 and the pressure is very much on. The Teignmouth sign can be seen resting on the hilltop, having just been sized on the as yet undetailed Sprey Point where a hand is resting. The east rough sea cassette is in position for the first time and Smugglers Lane Viaduct is being planned.

The rough sea cassette in position at the 2024 BRM Show. The waves crashing high against the sea wall are made from an old Santa's beard with layers of clear resin brushed through. The sea wall itself was engineered by member Brian Norris from insulative foam covered in scribed plaster, and then carefully painted with acrylics. (*Peachy TT:120, YouTube*)

Constructing the Cliffs

Exiting west from Parsons Tunnel on the mid afternoon of 31 August 1954 is the Torbay express from Paddington, having left at midday. The 4-6-0 Castle class 5097 *Lysander* (formerly *Lydford Castle*) is in charge of its chocolate and cream consist. Even at this early date, rough concrete defences have been placed below a wartime pillbox to protect the tunnel and cliff union from the waves. Making the famed cliffs appear real was the biggest challenge. (*Ben Brooksbank Geograph CC BY-SA 2.0 Deed*)

Where the cliffscape is concerned we had a number of build options. A traditional build would be a lightweight framework of wood and ply with netting pinned to it. An alternative, used before by the Club, would be card painted in PVA glue, or a plaster bandage, overlaying a former. Both these techniques are lightweight, and in smaller applications more than ideal. However, it was decided that combining strength, rigidity and an ability to sculpt to shape was desirable as the cliff and hill sections are demountable for show travel. Sheet insulation polystyrene was therefore chosen, and layers fixed with appropriate adhesive. We added pegs from barbecue skewers angled down through the formation, to ensure that the glue was not the only thing holding the layers in place.

The main unprofiled cliff in place along the line. As with most model railways, space is a constraint, therefore we chose several geological features representing the line approaching Teignmouth from the tunnel, portraying them in sequence. These include the change in the shade of the red rocks from a terracotta to the east, through to a more purple hue of the ex-desert Permian layers to the west. Colour is very important to a viewer, especially in an area of such note. Sprey Point to the front of the railway was chosen as a pivot point for all the features, and also provided a useful way of disguising the board joint.

Above left, above right, below left and below right: A kitchen knife could achieve much of the cliff cutting, but at the expense of static-rich polystyrene balls getting everywhere. Instead, we chose to use a single filament hot cutting probe sourced from eBay. One type of pollution replaces another: fumes. Bad weather precluded us working outside, so a vacuum cleaner with an extended tube acted as a fume extractor. Thus it was a two person job, one to melt through, the other to ensure we didn't all go home with sore throats. Once rough cut, the polystyrene was trimmed in more acute angles using a fret saw blade as a rasp.

The sweep of the east bay. A scenic break exists at both board joints, equating to our positioning of the major fault lines of the real geology. At the far end is Smugglers Lane, a deep cleft accessing the sea. Above Sprey Point is a rotative landslip that provided much of the original material for the promontory itself.

A solid polystyrene endpiece was burrowed through to form Parsons Tunnel at the east end of the beaches. This hides the curve to the fiddle yard and at the same time allows some impressive cliffscaping to be undertaken by the Club's latent geomorphologists. This is where the use of Sculptamold plaster allowed a hard finish to be sculpted and then carved. Poster or acrylic paint was then used to soak into the surface. This allowed for some future wear and tear to be hidden as shallow chips and scrapes would be self-coloured.

A *BBC Breakfast* news team in the Club room behind the beach and cliffscape. The media attendance at 6 am was in response to the closure of the long established Hattons model shop, and thoughts that the hobby was suffering a sharp decline. We were there to show the traditional hobby was still strong, but was also branching out into new technologies.

Right: Extreme tectonic activity! The west cliff and curve to Teignmouth station begins to get organic growth. Blends of differing type, colouration and density of scenic material were applied: static grass stuck in tufts, rubberised low shrub, with more traditional scatter material in between. The aim was to give the soft growth of early summer. Removable scenery meant we could do the messy parts in a controlled environment.

Below: Cliffs interrupt watercourses resulting in rivulets through to gorges. Here on the east cliff frontage a first layer of clear resin is painted into place to give the wet feel to ferns and moss that would grow there. If you logically follow your terrain and mark the lowest points, that is where your water will flow. In model form it looks right when you make the effort to get it correctly positioned.

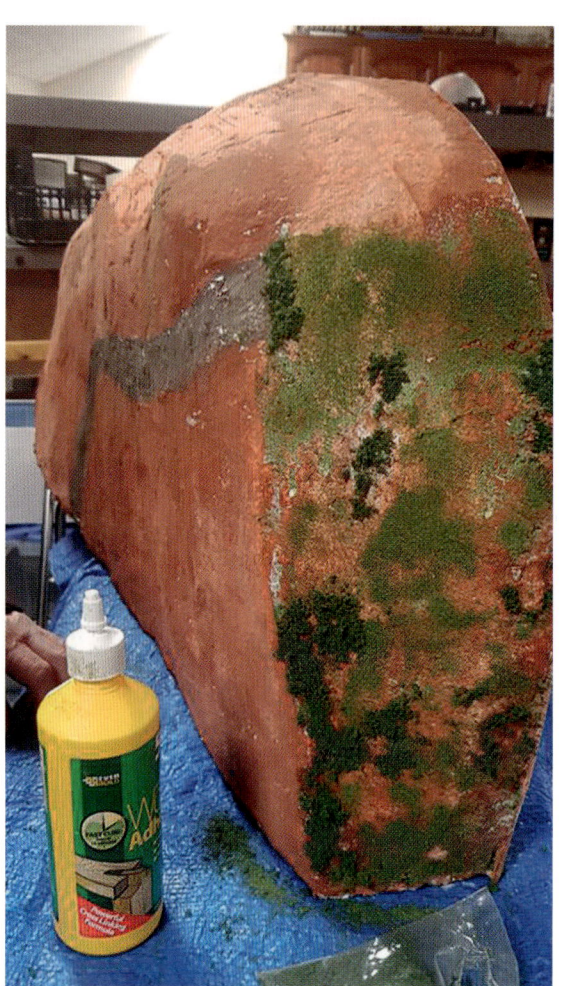

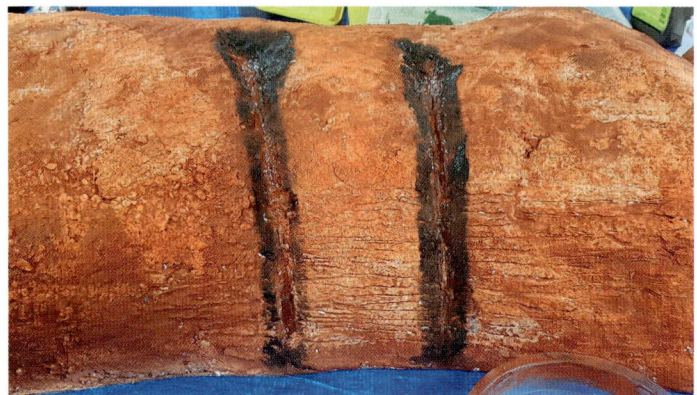

At this juncture the rest of the team were testing running rails, and beginning to ballast the trackbed. Track was sprayed first with a track dirt colour, then the rails were wiped clean with white spirit before the paint dried. The ballast was poured from a necked container, then brushed into position. Finally a 50% dilute PVA solution, with a drop of washing up liquid to break surface tension, was dripped over the top using a teat pipette. Note the colour light post which was made from an adapted tall N scale example by member Richard Elms, incorporating a new ladder to scale it up. This cleverly makes use of an electrical headphone style connector to allow it to be removed.

Above: The main cliff terracotta base colour was altered with red and purple tints to adjust to the real hues of the seaside rock face.

Right: This view of the rock exposure near Marine Parade in Dawlish shows the colouration aimed for in part of the Permian strata. Mainly stable, especially behind the railway, here Network Rail are adding some proactive consolidation to protect a footpath below.

Below: A bit like a bald man without his wig. As layers are added, field boundaries and road directions were planned, and size compromises made. A modeller can have doubts – if you get it wrong, scape it away and restart. We made several false starts (e.g. by holding images round the wrong way in the rush to meet the Doncaster 2024 show deadline).

The final blending of textures before the tree insertions began. Dilute PVA adhesive was brushed into place, then a dusting of basic green scatter materials added. Once that was dry another dabbing brush of dilute PVA was followed by pinches of static grass. We did not use a static grass applicator, since a rough, tufted finish was required.

Selected photographs from the internet were used for tree planting guidance. These included satellite and drone shots as well as general tourist shots made public. The scenic backing boards were painted by artist member Graham Hobbs once roads and major woodland had been established.

YouTube and magazine content being created for *BRM*. In this case Phil Parker, editor of *Garden Rail* and features writer for *BRM* (also co-moderator of RMweb), is taking images and conducting interviews with the team. This formed a series of YouTube documentaries to demonstrate the techniques used, and show the overall progress of the sponsored project.

THE SEAFRONT • 55

The BRM show, Doncaster, 10 February 2024. The BR blue Class 08 heads a newly released set of tankers straight out the box, along the calm seafront. A control chip, 'stay alive' battery and sound cube add a little extra to the weight of the loco. Although it has dependable adhesion qualities, there is a danger of overheating in long use. Eventually the advertised Class 50 from Hornby would be available to make this closer to prototypical services. The sandy, calm beach blends in well. Recognise the two defiles coming down the cliff face from earlier?

The full sinuous frontage of the challenge layout with our morning display of calm seas. The irregular wave patterns and colour gradient used work well in overall context with the vibrant palette of the south Devon riviera cliffscape. The mouth of Parsons Tunnel was specially commissioned, and is now available commercially.

Again at BRM Doncaster. Seen from atop the tunnel as freight and passenger pass each other at Sprey Point. Santa's beard offcuts were reinforced by the transparent resin of the Making Waves product. The highest points of the spume were then highlighted in white gloss enamel paint. (*Peachy TT:120,. YouTube*)

The tight deadline for this project made for a speedy build. Some components were worked on at home, while others were created in windows of a few hours on Club nights. We had to seek solutions to problems quickly. For example, the 3D resin printing of the Teignmouth sign had a size limitation in terms of the print bath. To get round this, the computer model was rotated and skewed to fit the maximum possible size for a single print. This meant ensuring that there were supports attached to allow the soft material to maintain print position before UV light curing. These were cut away after. Each area of cliff, sea wall, bridge and woodland had printed images and details for us to follow. This ensured that the finished model looked cohesive. The steps to the sea are a great example of a testbed later being used on the model itself. The steps and 3D-printed railings demonstrate the attention to detail when compared to the site image. Member Brian Norris was responsible for this and the sea wall. (*Brian Norris*)

5
The HSTs Arrive

The Inter City 125, otherwise known as the High Speed Train (HST), came into production in 1976. It represented a significant development in British railway history, combining speed, safety and reliability. Originally each power car was equipped with a Paxman Valenta engine, giving a very recognisable turbine whine when leaving the station. Each of the 95 sets assembled for the Western and Eastern Regions had a Class 43 power car at each end, and seven or eight Mark 3 coaches. Seen here on a cold Easter morning at Paddington (07:30 on 3 April 1980), power cars 253026 and 253025 are preparing for departure. In the middle, 253024 has just drifted in empty stock. The TT:120 HST models arrived at the Club just prior to our own May 2024 Stamford show. To the project members this was a 'red letter day' for the Dawlish (by now more accurately renamed *Holcombe Beach*) model. At last we had the correct passenger stock for the required cameo date.

Our first public event. Production and delivery of the HST sets was running late with just the prototypes in the UK. What to do? To the rescue, YouTuber Peachy TT:120 with an ICE train of UK pattern to test our track sweeps.

The Inter City Swallow liveried set passes Sprey Point at speed towards Teignmouth, with the afternoon storm scene cassette inserted. In common with the ICE train previously used at the Doncaster exhibition, a full length consist in this scale, replete with sound chip engines and horns blaring, is a great experience.

At rest. Ready for the first full rake test with replacement magnetic couplings in place.

Looking east from the premises of the Teign Corinthian Yacht Club, one can see the recurves of the track frontage working well with the long Mark 3 coaches. As they have a little more dead weight than Mark 1s they remained firmly on the track on the tighter curves to the fiddle yard at the rear. Derailment of greater than five Mark 1 coaches on a steam special presented a problem to the team when operating, so they needed some carful weighting.

Right: Examples of the Mark 3 coaches, all with couplings replaced with West Hill Wagon Works magnets.

Below: Soon after this, the Class 50 'Hoover' was released. Here DCC sound 50 007 *Sir Edward Elgar* exits Teignmouth station with a brake gangwayed (BG) support coach. The sound file for this locomotive is very 'throaty'.

The Swallow Executive livery HST. In common with the 1970s' livery variant, the Club models came without control and sound chipping or a 'stay alive' battery. These required fitting, and our friend Chris from the Peachy TT:120 YouTube channel came to the rescue, providing a 'how to do it' sequence. (*Peachy TT:120, YouTube*)

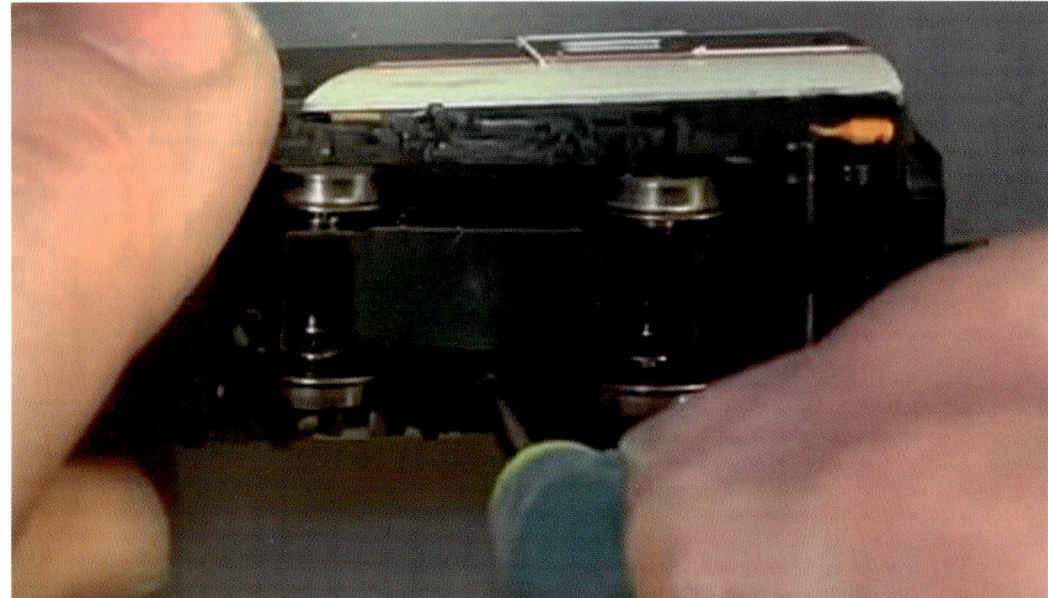

As per the instructions, the first requirement is to get a screwdriver between the bogies and bogie detailing plate. A pair of long screws are removed at each end. Look after these for later replacement. (*Peachy TT:120, YouTube*)

You then need to tease a pair of chassis clips from the body at the guard's end of the power car. Wiggle gently – it will pivot down, allowing the nose end to be pulled out. (*Peachy TT:120, YouTube*)

THE HSTs ARRIVE • 61

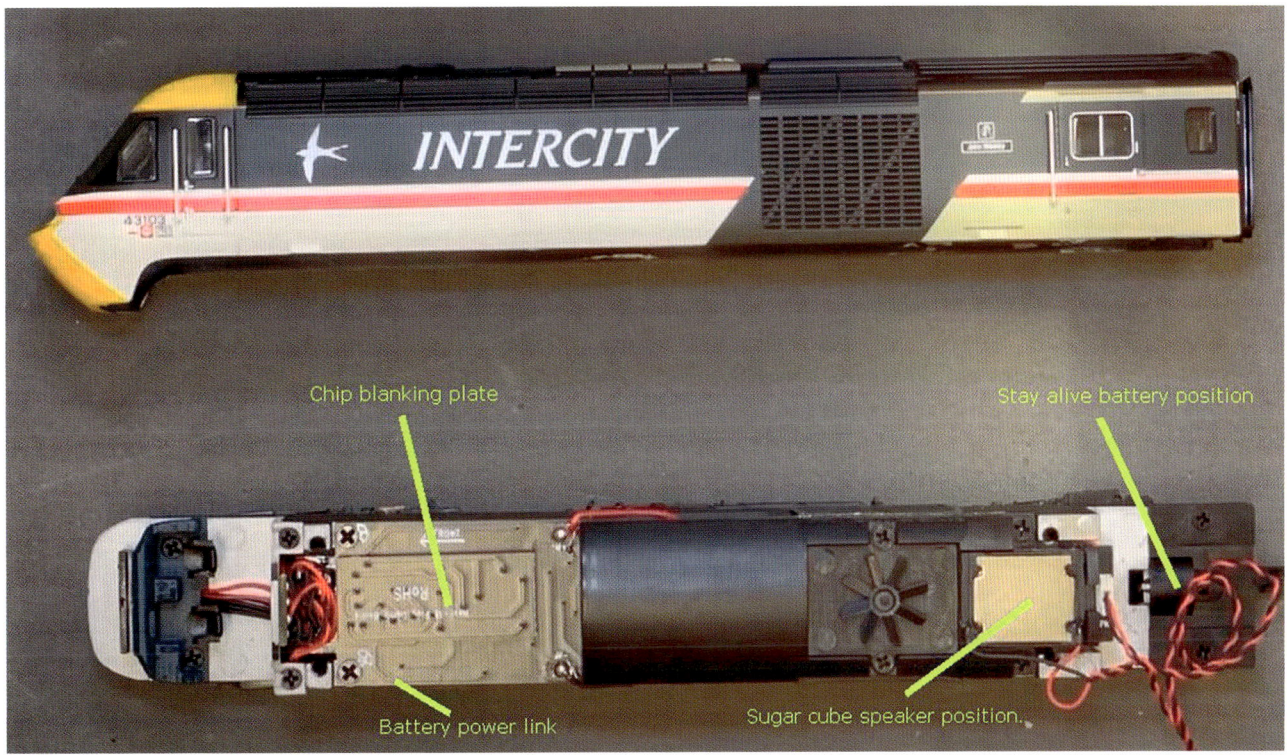

The 'plug and play' chip port of the locomotive is protected by a blanking plate at the cab end. A sugar-cube speaker has just been added next to the fan detail. Although there is a lot of wire, it is best left in its original length. The only space for a 'stay alive' battery is inside the guard's compartment at the far end. This will connect to the chip board at the other end. (*Peachy TT:120, YouTube*)

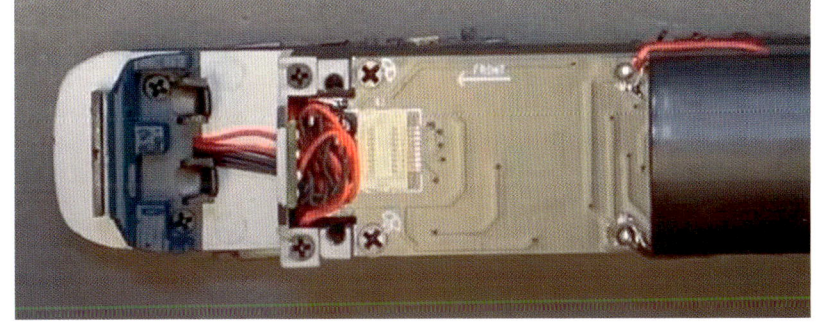

The chip port blanking plate has been removed here, a simple lifting process. (*Peachy TT:120, YouTube*)

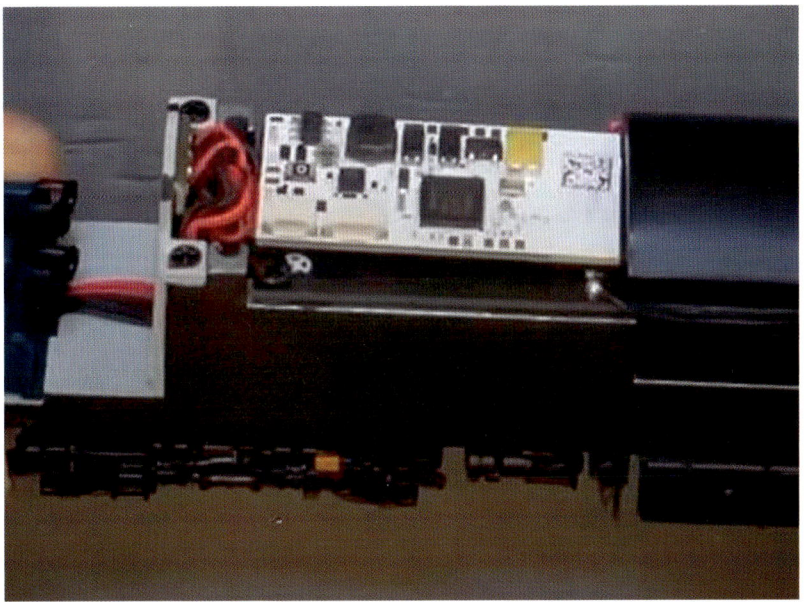

The HM7000 chip is then pushed gently into place. It should not give much resistance. If pressing from above, ensure the anti-static plastic that the chip came in is used as a barrier for protection. (*Peachy TT:120, YouTube*)

The power bank for the 'stay alive' battery is plugged into the chip set. The red and black motor power wires are run along a shelf at the top of the inner body. (*Peachy TT:120, YouTube*)

Left: An insulating tape cover is placed over to retain wire position. As there is side detailing for the radiator, this is cut out with a craft knife. The power bank itself may need some heat shrink insulation trimmed away to get it into position. Black Tack adhesive putty is used to adhere the battery array to the chassis. (*Peachy TT:120, YouTube*)

Below: Finally, with the power pack squeezed in place the body can be reintroduced into position, dipping the chassis into the nose cone and reclipping. Don't forget the four long screws as a finishing task. The desired DCC address can then be coded into the chip. There is the capability of chipping and sound cubing the alternate end power car (unmotored) so it also provides a sound output. That becomes a financial decision. On a correct length train, having both sound sources go past does add to the overall realism. (*Peachy TT:120, YouTube*)

6
The Alternative Challenge – *Black Bridge*

When Hornby released steam-age East Coast Main Line (ECML) rolling stock in TT:120, such as the A3 *Night Hawk*, it was hard to resist choosing a location to showcase it, in the form of an alternative 'challenge' layout. We went for Bedlington Viaduct or the 'Black Bridge', near Blythe in Northumberland. Originally this was a wooden structure, and today it carries a freight-only line. Currently there is hope for the return of passengers between Newcastle and Morpeth. We wanted to produce something relatively easy to build, taking advantage of 3D printing to broaden the availability of accessories.

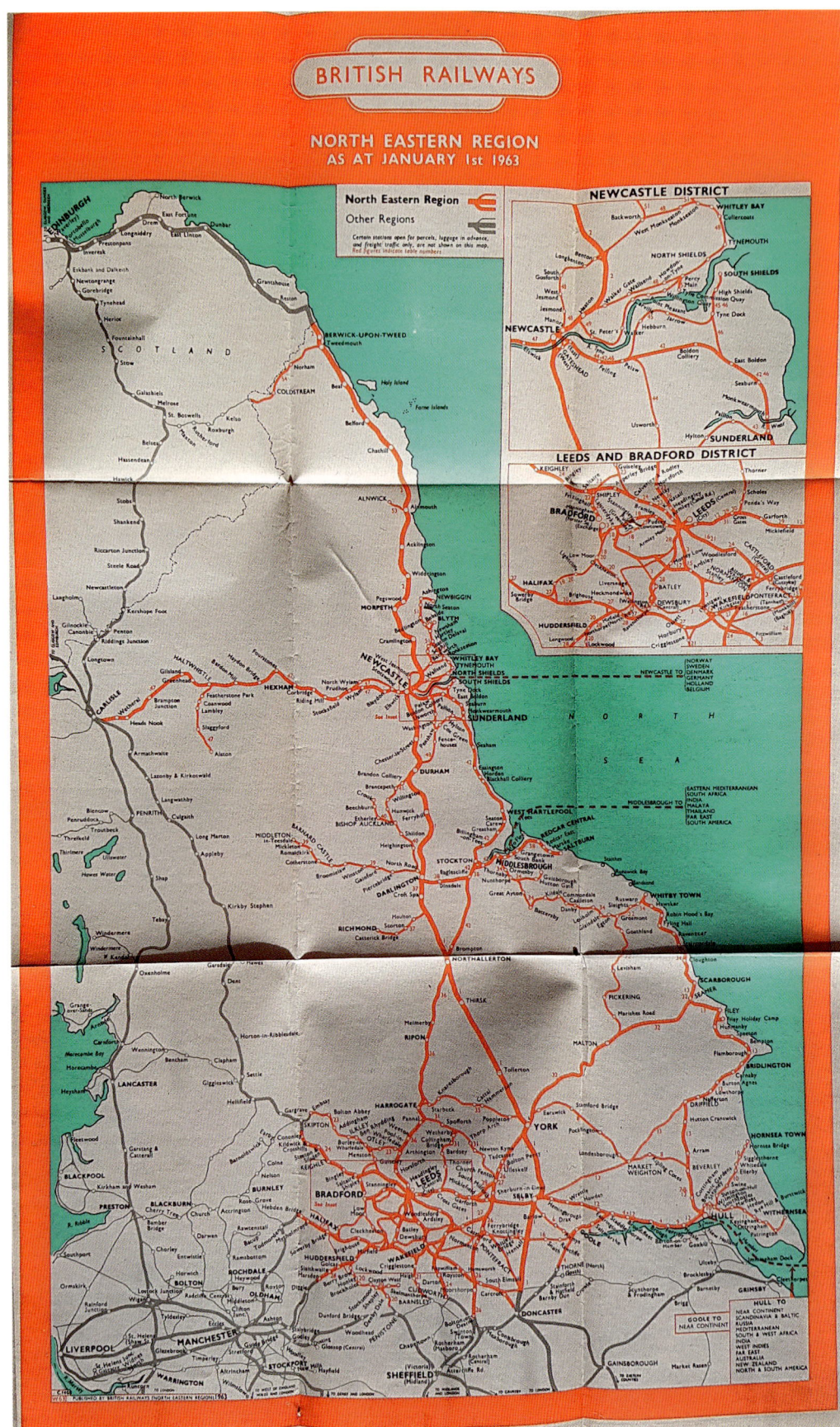

The North Eastern Region of British Railways, home of the tangerine-orange hue of enamel signage in the 1950s and 60s. The North Eastern Railway maintained its identity after the 1948 nationalisation, forming a network over an industrial heartland based on coal, steel and shipbuilding. No matter what period or location a modeller chooses, background resources such as maps, charts, timetables, picture and history books all add to the authenticity of the model and overall satisfaction. (*Author's collection*)

A Shunter Interlude

Our parallel project in TT:120, a layout called *Black Bridge*, coincided with the first deliveries of TT products, one of which was a model of 08 shunter no. 489. When this arrived we were able to use it to determine 'true scale'. Back in the 1960s/70s, when plastic injection moulding was making itself useful on the railway modelling market, it was expected that there would be a one-size-fits-all principle. The research and development into a product and the cost of making the injection moulds meant that prototype changes over time were rarely reflected, other than in the form of aftermarket detailing to be undertaken personally. We must say that the 08 model runs extremely well at low speeds, and since we have a 'stay alive' battery fitted, there are no worries at all over rougher joints or point frogs. It can also pull a decent load! Paint and print cannot be faulted even under close scrutiny.

The later build representations also incorporate prototype differences for the

Many of us have favourite locomotives, often from early spotting or shed visit days. In the case of the author it is the ubiquitous Class 08 shunter. A cold winter's day in 1980 led to dropping into Old Oak Common from the Grand Union Canal footbridge access, mainly to get out the wind. Here three unidentified 'Gronks' were tucked away in the fuelling/service shed.

purists. For example, 08 849 has a single door handle on the cab and square windows, whereas 08 818 (see the GBRf number 4 in the image) has rounded windows and the door handle repeater at the base. Note also the extra battery box and reduced ventilation grill space. We replaced the coupling at one end with a magnetic coupler for our own stock upgrades, but left the original at the B end for working with visiting stock. If you ever need to get to the conrod bolts you will ideally need tool TT8038. DCC chipping can be considered, but to squeeze in a control chip, a 'stay alive' battery and a speaker it would be best to go the professional route for fitting.

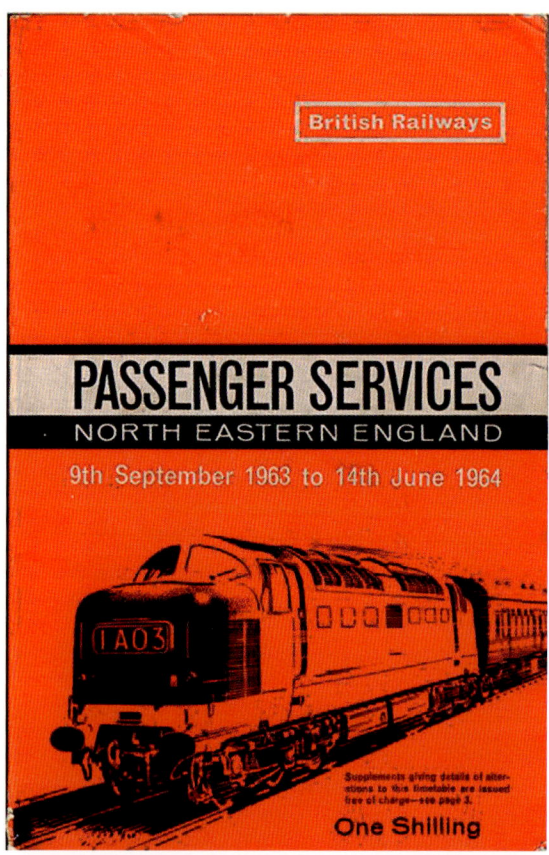

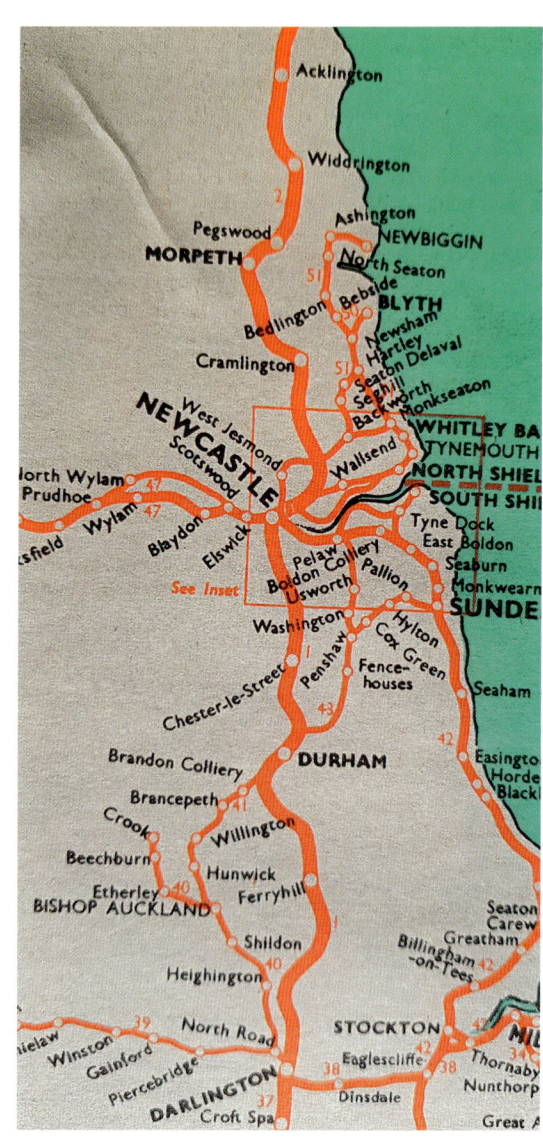

Above and right: One of the first actions when a subject location is chosen is to get a deeper understanding of its context in the landscape, its history and the physical railway. In this case, we purchased several contemporary guides, timetables and gazetteers. In our minds, the Bedlington and Blyth line could have formed a Morpeth bypass joining Ashington to Widdrington. This would mean that when engineering was taking place, the main line services could have been diverted over the Bedlington Viaduct. (*Author's collection*)

Having a totem or other signage made up for your layout can seem a costly extra, however, many shows have a trader who can make these up as a vinyl overlay on a plastic substrate, while you wait. Much cheaper than a replica enamel sign, or indeed going to an auction for an original. This example was created by Ron Connor Signs ('The Totem Man') at the 2024 Stamford Show.

One walks around with a model railway requirement in the head for a few weeks and suddenly inspiration hits. In this case some raised flower beds were needed, which would make use of the steel-hinged corners of the bed frame kit, but not the timber. That wood met the constructional requirement for depth and weight for the *Black Bridge* project. So we now had a baseboard kit of pre-cut size, as a byproduct of another project.

No matter how much effort you put into a track plan, never be afraid to amend it based on operational ideas, changes in technical setup, availability of new products and suchlike. Just prior to execution of the dual main line which was to present a general scenic sweep rather like that of *Holcombe Beach*, the thought came along: why have two layouts the same?

A station was needed. Off-the-shelf kits for eastern prototypes now exist and could be used. The scheme would need to have a refuge siding and goods yard. So then the signal box position became a station siding headshunt – it looks good to have buffers before a steep drop. What was the entrance of a colliery line to a staithe became a peek-a-boo reveal of shunter and wagons through a low-relief factory unit. A turntable idea proved too fiddly in this iteration, so the coal drops appear set back in its place. This layout is a bit more traditional, but with DCC control, there is far more shunting to keep interest going at exhibitions, and to provide general playtime. The 3D-printed signal box is thus placed to the right-hand side of the viaduct, and a new one such as that produced by Hornby for TT:120 will be positioned to the left of the board at the station exit.

The train now standing ... Static locomotive models exist for TT:120 from the Corgi range. These examples were sourced from eBay and are a great way to cheaply populate the MPD, and a 3D-printed turntable that will appear in *Black Bridge* phase 2. Here, displaying the early British Rail lion-on-wheel totem, 70000 *Britannia* is ready for detachment and shed allocation. Some brave modellers have attempted working chassis conversions with these locomotives.

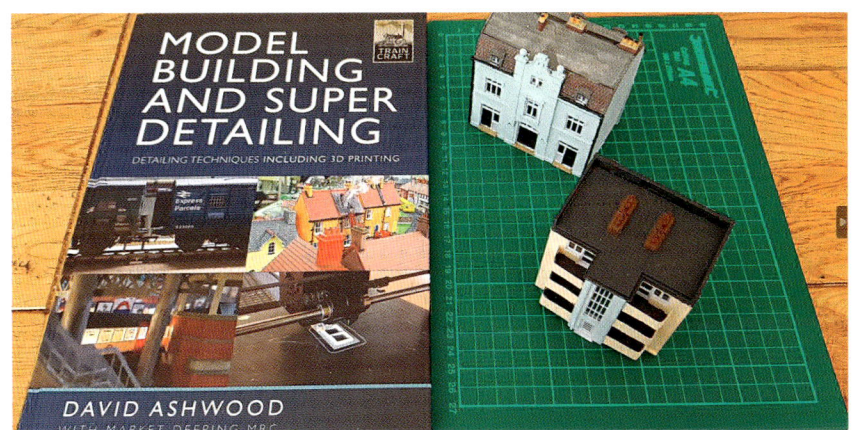

Holcombe Beach was to have a few scratch-built landmark buildings. For *Black Bridge*, however, a small town was to be created, but at the inception of TT:120 there was very little on the market to achieve this. So enter 3D printing with rescaling of pre-existing model designs for other scales. Techniques such as this are covered in our third book, *Model Building and Super Detailing* (Pen and Sword 2024).

A similar issue existed with rolling stock. We needed some dummies for TT:120 to fill in exchange and coal drop sidings at the back of the layout. Instead of paying a premium for the few wagon styles that existed, we located a free flat printable kit. Now we were able to make the backscene look busy at about £1 a wagon. If you have a deeper layout, you can force perspective by using N scale at the back

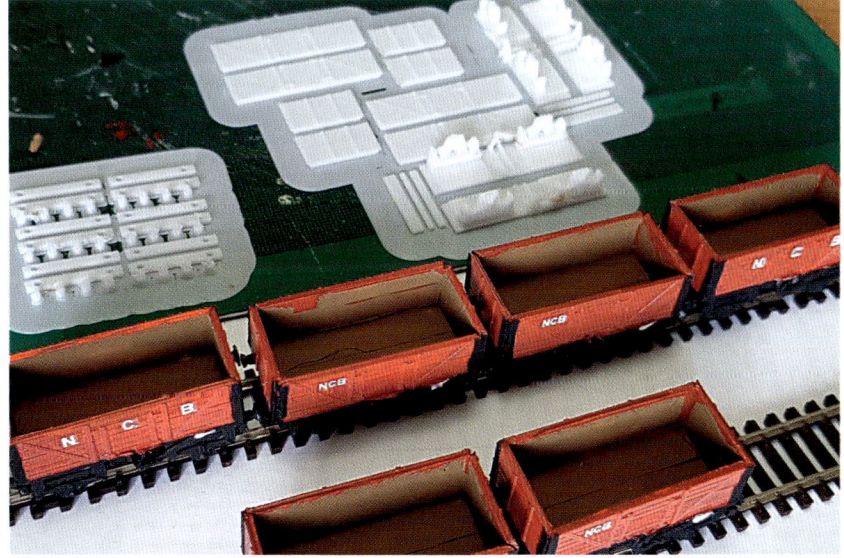

A lesson learned from the other layout build was to move to a magnetic coupling system on all rolling stock. This was for a combination of stability and ease of separation. New technology means that both poles of the magnet are exposed on the same coupling face – no more turning wagons to match north to south pole.

7
The Viaduct Build

Concrete beams destined for the Ash Vale Station Approach road bridge over the Basingstoke Canal, being shipped on 22 January 1989. Over the years, materials for bridges and viaducts have evolved through wood, stone and brick, to wrought iron and steel, then pre-stressed concrete assemblies from specialist factories. The viaduct chosen for *Black Bridge* was originally a substantial wooden affair, replaced by the LNER with steel trusswork. (*Online Transport Archive: Meredith-1152-4 – BR*)

The railways of the north-east of England made extensive use of wooden structures for staithes and viaducts. This model on the waterfront at Blyth shows the complex structure of the extensive Cambois staithes, made famous by the chase with Michael Caine in the film *Get Carter*.

Seeking a Muse

A site visit, should such be possible, can yield much detail that could be missed from other people's photographs. As well as filling the mind-space of the modeller with a multisensory knowledge of the location (including smell), the photographic evidence gathered is personalised.

Although prototype photographs give the overall target for a modeller, seeing how others have presented a certain feature can be an inspiration. One of the joys of going around a model railway show is witnessing the differing techniques presented – all of which make sense in their context – and wondering if they could be utilised to one's own advantage.

Because TT:120 is so fresh on the scene, there are few display models at present, so any scale can contribute to the repository of ideas at the back of the mind. There was no doubt that the spidery Bedlington Viaduct would have to be a compromise in length and height. That left us with the challenge of portraying the feel of a dominant structure, confined within a single board segment. Our fellow exhibition colleagues came to the rescue.

The 4mm/OOn9 *Tarrant Valley Railway* by Wimborne Railway Society has water features that achieve the same overall effect but use very different techniques. The River Tarrant in the trestle bridge picture is made from a clear resin. Movement is depicted by surface ripples, likely made by blowing cool air at an angle as the resin began final setting. It catches the overhead lighting well, giving the impression of lively movement between the riverbank growth.

While the oxbow meander by the station uses the same deep grey/blue base colour for consistency, the surface makes use of successive layers of varnish instead of resin. Although the U-boat conning tower is a nice fun touch, the use of floating swans provides a real feeling of depth and realism.

Our own *Canons Cross* layout has a narrow defile with a canal running towards the viewer. Since the rails run over the tunnel at the rear there is a general reveal to the viewer. In a similar manner the tidal river section being modelled for *Black Bridge*, despite being foreshortened, could draw the viewer beyond the actual viaduct structure.

On the Club *North Cape, Kimberley* layout, we introduced a single line over a river viaduct in South Africa, a mock-up of which can be seen here. It was designed to pull the eye through to the backscene, in turn illuminated by light of varying colours and intensity. If you have doubts with regards to personal build skills, some 'offline' practice on a small diorama such as this always serves to boost confidence.

Scarlington in N gauge by Nick Skelton and the Noel Group of Railway Modellers. N allows you to fit a lot in, to tremendous impact, as shown here with the Tyne bridged over.

Monkchester, also in N, from the Newcastle Model Railway Club. The valley forms here gave confidence for the River Blyth build approach. Here a plateau is cut by deep valleys, and the lines also dive into tunnels to hide return curves from the viewer. The same technique would be used to recurve to the fiddle yard on *Black Bridge*.

The Bedlington Viaduct in 2023. Steelwork replaced the original timber structure in 1930 and the infrastructure is looking good today. Alternative names are Blythe Bridge, Kitty Brewster Bridge or the Black Bridge. Despite being a somewhat compact river valley cut down into a plateau, the modelled viaduct still had to be reduced in size to fit the available space when allocated to a single board in TT:120.

Above: The footing of the central spans of the structure is situated in the tidal River Blythe. The river here is not navigable and shows a good variation from full flood to mud flats, with murky spring silt in the water. No remains of the foundations of the original timber viaduct could be located.

Right: Lovers of Meccano will enjoy this image. The overall construction is a delicate tracery of steelwork, not the massive plate steel of smaller bridges.

The B1131 going under the Bedlington Viaduct northern span. Having a road featured alongside the river assists the 'pull' of the eye to beyond the front scene. This site visit took place before the reinstatement of passenger services on this line.

The legs of the viaduct slot neatly into the deck of the railbed. This means a snug fit in terms of model construction. Since the track will run over an uncut section of the baseboard connecting the two sides, we would need some stability and stiffening, so this prototype design would allow the model to reflect real-life requirements.

With the boards covered in ply, radii for returns to fiddle yard worked out, and the boards bolted together, the project started. As usual, four-legged supervision of humans was provided, this time by a kitten called Hollie.

The chosen module, measured and cut to profile for the river valley. The trackbed plywood has been retained to make the finished viaduct strong for transit. At the rear is the position of the return fiddle yard for the circuit, where the scenic break will be placed at the head of the valley. The rear valley profile was taken from the front cutout and plywood for the riverbed stapled and glued in place.

The trusty Class 08 posed as the first supporting tower is constructed from 3D-printed elements. We cover such print techniques in our third book, *Model Building and Super Detailing* (Pen and Sword 2024). The chicken-wire mesh of the valley sides could also have been made using a cardboard weave, a tried and tested technique.

Above left and above right: Although you can design your own elements from scratch for 3D printing use, you can also purchase pre-made plans or find free-to-use examples on such websites as www.thingiverse.com. This is a reuse of a plate bridge free design, where the three axis measurements have been set to TT:120 scale.

Above and right: Fun for all the family. The author's granddaughter enjoying getting artistic. Laying Modroc plaster sheets over a stapled and sculpted chicken-wire substrate is a middle-school type activity, as is painting details such as the viaduct sides. Pre-plan and agree tasks. Remember that attention spans for youngsters are short – they always have been, it's just we forget with time.

As a terrain base, polystyrene was contemplated and rejected, since too much micro-variation was required. Plaster rolls are very good for building up a strong base layer, and have been used by generations of railway modellers. The combination of wire and cloth is very lightweight, a bonus in a portable layout.

THE VIADUCT BUILD • 77

Brushing with PVA glue solution to ensure the join between Modroc bandage and plywood has a strong bond.

For 'terrain capping' (far left and right), polystyrene *was* used, the pieces having been rescued from product packaging

The trackbed now has a double layer of thin cork, which is both sound absorbent and enables a decent ballast profile to be made. The long frontage of display tracks made use of Peco flexible track sections.

More 'back to school' fun, using acrylic paints to build a colour profile in the scenic area of the valley. Although most of this will be covered by subsequent scatter and static grass material, a colour base such as this helps give a depth of finish.

Approaching the endgame for this part of the layout. A3 60078 *Night Hawk* passes slowly on a test train. More scenic density with trees is planned to the rear, and when combined with a final cloud-painted backscene this will complete the viaduct module. Overall, a fun build. *Black Bridge* will hopefully soon be enhanced by the appearance of the new Gresley J50 tank locomotive in LNER black from Hornby.

Actually a guest star on *Holcombe Beach* while on display at BRM Doncaster 2024, certainly something to aspire to. A Mallard model conversion by YouTuber Peachy TT:120 into wartime 4498 *Sir Nigel Gresley*. This was more than a re-livery, having leading and trailing LED lights added. The 'how to', and much more useful information, are available on his online channel.

8
Control Options

A 'second man' seat view of the line ahead at Fleet, 5 August 1965. The signal ahead is clear. What at that time was a state of the art unit with engine, braking and safety controls improving on the generation before, is about to draw off. With DCC now giving the model railway owner a viable alternative to the long established DC control, we cover some options for powering TT:120 models in this chapter. (*Online Transport Archive: AND-M566-1*)

Above: Tempting as it may be to be modern and reuse old control units, the motors of TT:120 locomotives and associated chip sets require a modern control system without the dangers of power spikes, earthing deficiencies and overheating. Seen here in the Club museum collection is a walk-through 12V history, all now consigned to viewing only as they would probably not pass a modern PAT (portable appliance test). Meccano, the H&M Clipper … happy days!

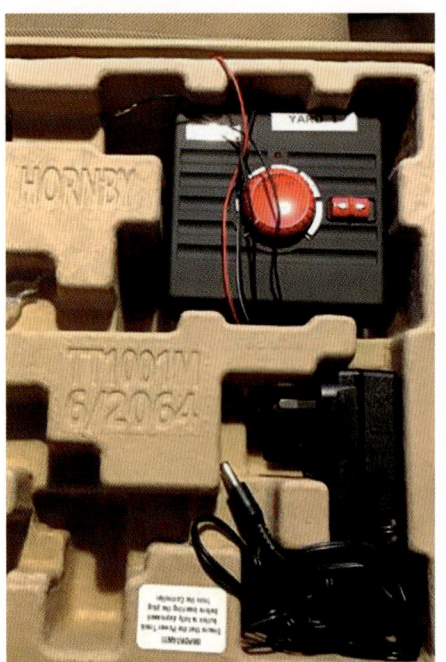

Left and below: If you buy the basic TT:120 train sets without chip control and sound, you receive a simple directional controller fed from a separate transformer. This will provide for single locomotive operation and prevent younger hands from doing the skidding forward and backward motion in play which wrecks the more modern locomotives. If more than one circuit and controller are wanted, then judicious isolation between them will result in two circuits in operation without many issues. You can finesse things with other higher-quality makes of analogue controller, with a nicer hand interface, smoother slow movement, and even simulated braking. The first commissioning tests of the TT:120 *Holcombe Beach* layout used simple DC, since the locomotives were chipped later.

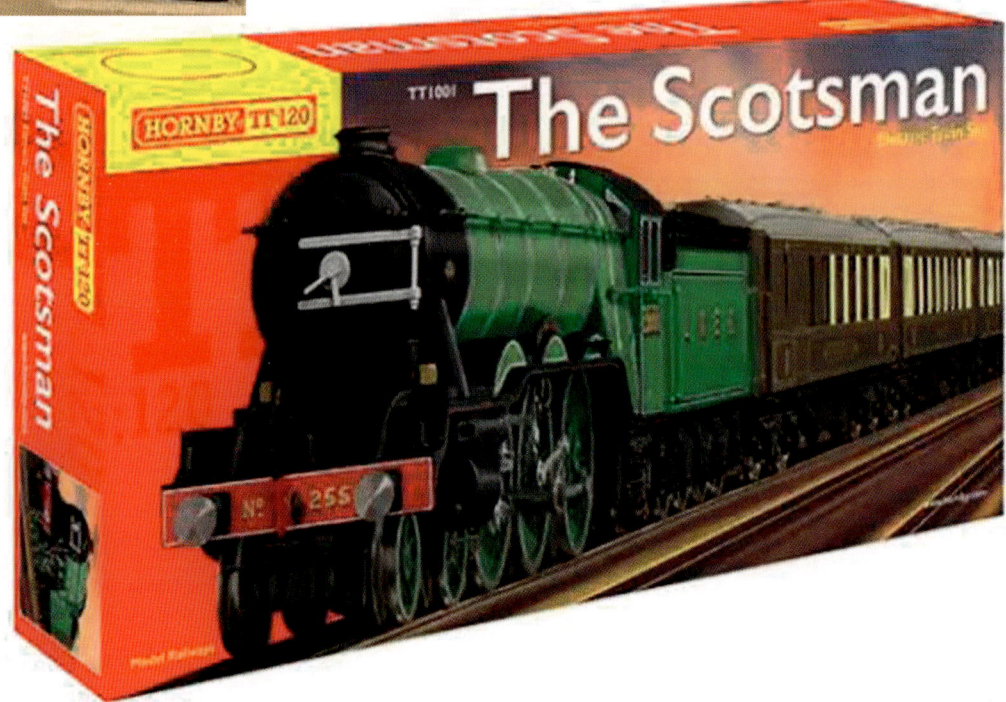

CONTROL OPTIONS • 81

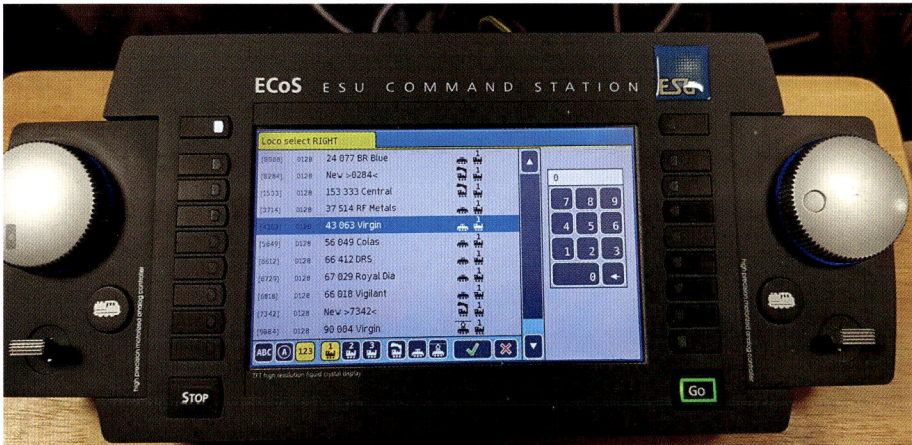

Above, left and below: The ECOS ESU Command Station being piloted on the Club TT:120 and OO layouts. Here twin cab controls are seen along with graphical locomotive allocation and the ability to use icons to trigger specific sounds on the chip set rather than an anonymous function key setting. The open, graphic look and feel enabled members of all ages to participate quickly.

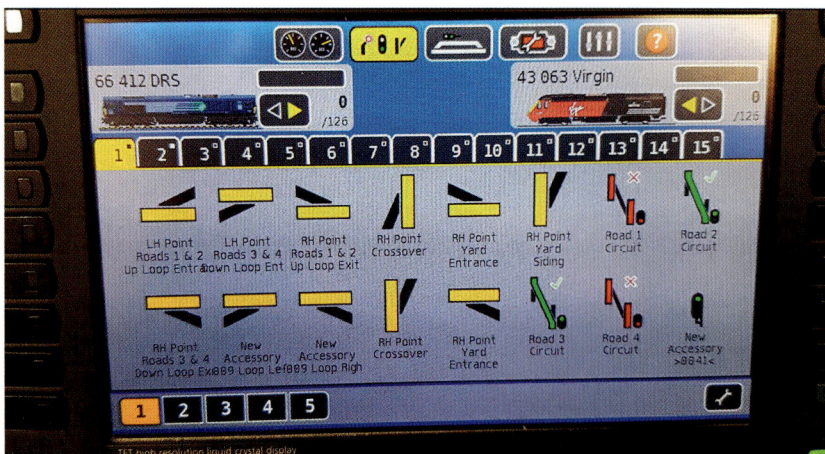

Once all turnouts and signals have been programmed there is the ability to create single settings selecting combinations for a defined route. This emulates the prototype practice of the old power signal box, through to today's digital signalling centre.

The layout shown here is the Club's *Mitchell Junction* in OO, giving an idea of the capability of the ECOS system. Because the *Holcombe Beach* TT:120 layout was kept as simple as possible, route selection would just represent two turnouts in combination for the fiddle yard. Our twinned hard wiring already covered this requirement.

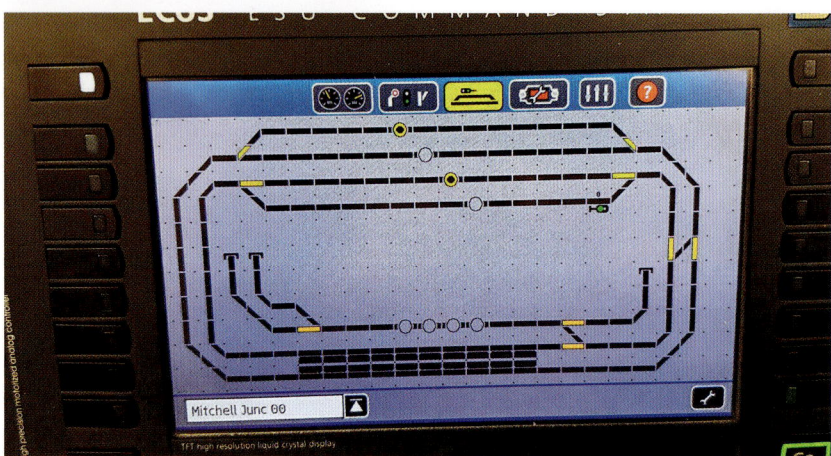

Proven in action and the chosen backup system for use at outside events is the NCE Power Cab DCC system. A single handset can control both directions on a layout such as *Holcombe Beach*.

A challenge can be remembering the chip addresses of locomotives and accessories. For a loco, we take first two and final two digits of the cab number. Thus 50 007 becomes address 5007 to allocate the loco. For accessories we have a handy label on the scenic backing to remind us which numbers cover lights and points.

CONTROL OPTIONS • 83

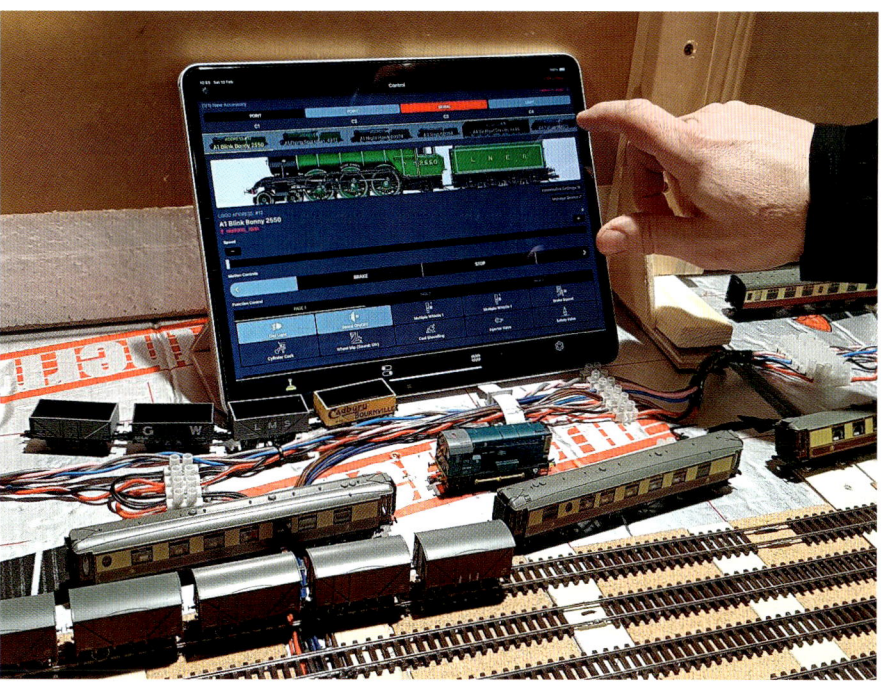

Right and below: At the Doncaster BRM show in 2024 we had YouTube guest star Peachy TT:120 join us for the two days. We were able to test drive the HM9000 tablet-based software with the Hornby dedicated control. Effectively blue-toothing to a paired locomotive, it is another way of providing that extra interface, and the ability to walk and talk at the same time. We had the points and signals hard wired for NCE, so had to retain that for other controls.

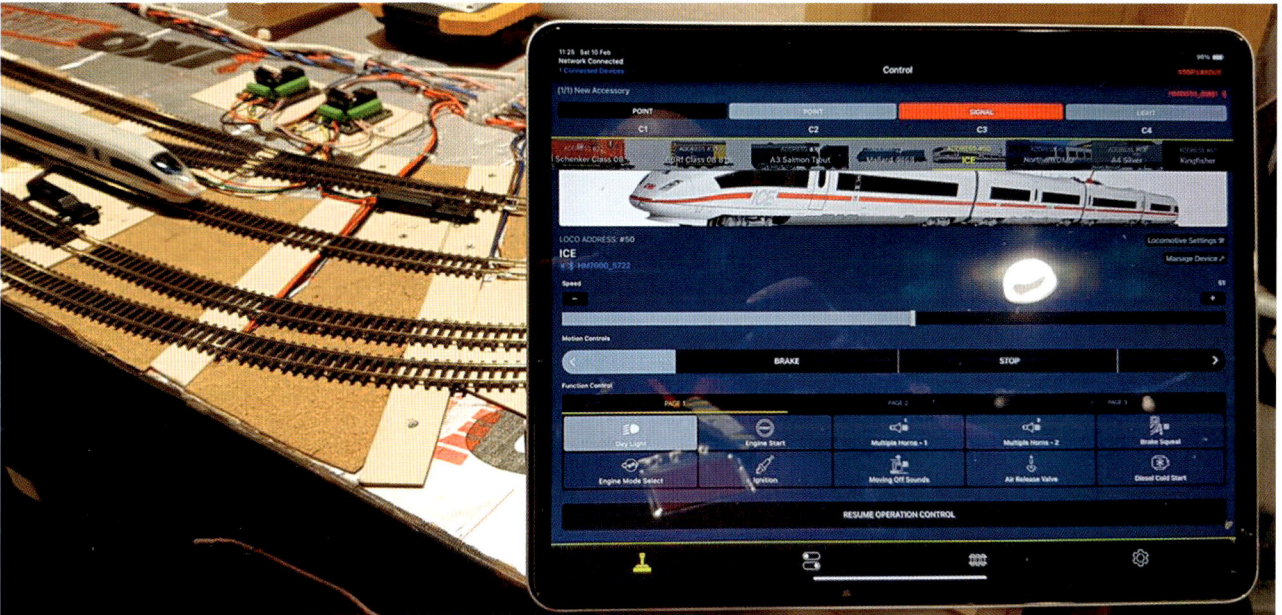

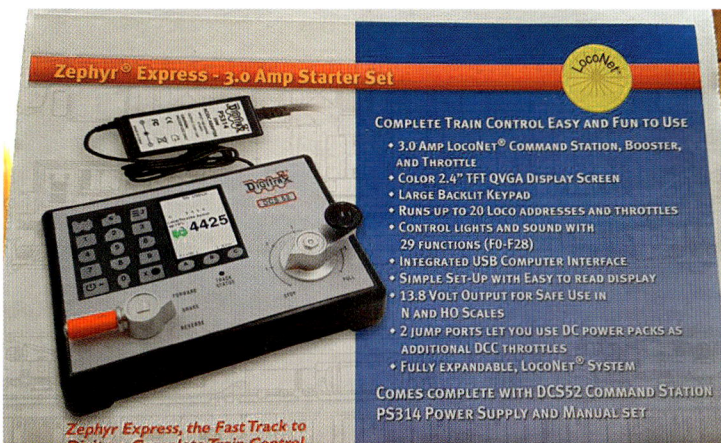

Above left and above right: Dare to be different. The author chose his own Zephyr Express system for use on *Black Bridge*, mainly because of personal preference: the interface felt nicer than NCE, plus that layout is worked from a fixed location.

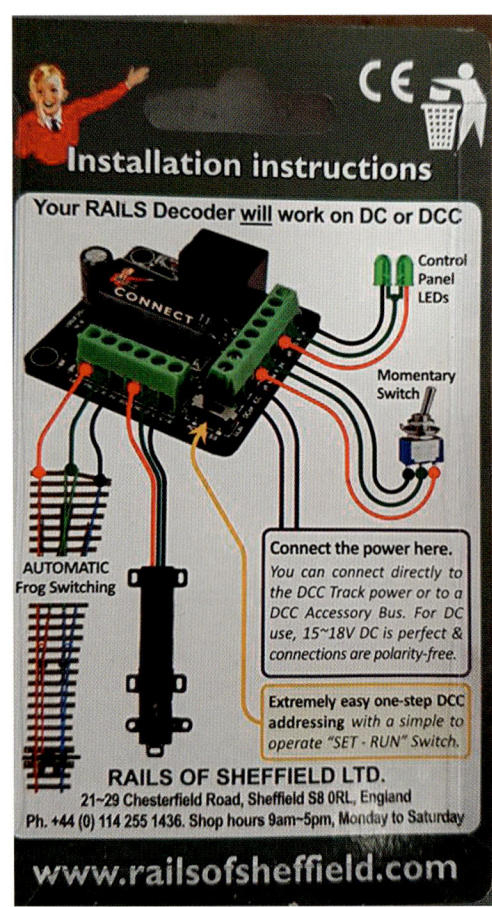

Left and above: The turnout control chosen for *Holcombe Beach* was that from Rails of Sheffield. It has only medium complexity and a decent price point. For all the fiddle yard turnouts we were surface mounting the motors on top of the foam baseboard. One unforeseen challenge was overcome – the need for a shim on the connection point itself, so that the motor drive would have a tight fit.

Anyone who says DCC is 'just two wires' is underestimating things. While the wires from control to accessory destination can be a twisted pair, the accessory to the executional element has to be wired in. We put in two power sources, one for the running lines, the other for accessories. Not a prerequisite, but a choice to ensure clean supply for all requirements.

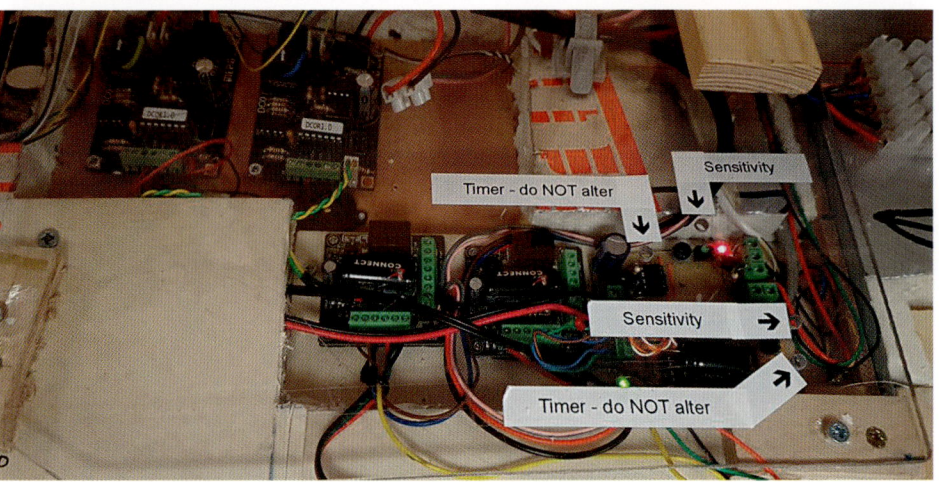

Eventually our controls were sunk into the face of the foam baseboard, mining out a hole and facing it with fine ply. Topping with Perspex allowed access to tuning points, and protected the rest of the equipment.

9
Lighting

Broad Street Station, the terminus of the North London Railway, was always regarded as a dull and difficult-to-photograph location. The dirty canopy and poor lighting, as well as limited subject matter, made it a rare subject for pictures. In the final days before redevelopment, the overall roof was removed and there was better opportunity to take images of trains bound for Richmond or Watford via Dalston Junction. Seen here in the shadows in June 1984 are two class 416 units, with the then new 183m tall Tower 42, or Nat West Tower, behind. Lighting a model railway layout is important – it provides ambience. With modern LED technology the ability to change from summer to winter, amend weather conditions and highlight or hide things can be a game-changer. (*B. Mulquin, GWRPG Collection*)

So why is a minor weather-related gazebo disaster being shown here? The answer is upcycling. A mix of steel struts, PVC fixings and uprights that so often would go straight into the bin. The remains didn't take up much room, so the idea of a universal lighting rig that could be used on *Black Bridge* and other layouts such as our O gauge *Butterwick*, came to fruition.

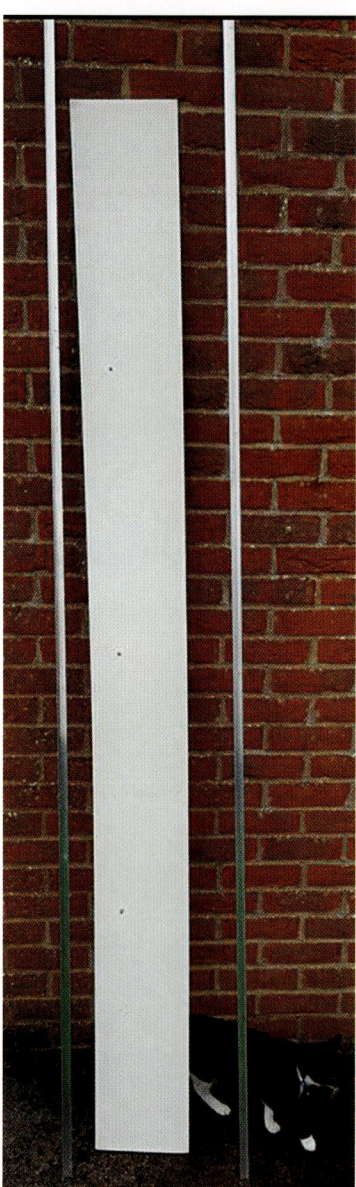

A rescued UPVC sofit panel was next on the recycle list, Hollie the cat for scale. Angled aluminium struts, spare from making rolling stock cassettes, were an ideal stiffener for this. After thorough cleaning the pieces were held together using double-sided tape and some short bolts. Dispose of the drilled swarf carefully.

Above: The gazebo was disassembled and the fittings put into the traditional mix of jars and tins. A pair of uprights and some cross spars were readied for drilling and bolting.

Right: A simple cantilever is all that is needed. With a weight on the feet and a G-cramp on the upright, we have a robust variable-height assemblage.

Below: Two colour-adjustable LED self-adhesive strip lighting kits were procured from the 'middle of Lidl'. The quality of these strip kits has improved over the years. These are for kitchen use with the strip encased in soft plastic, ideal for the rough handling that a lighting array can have in transit. The strips were halved, linked and alternated with a control box at either end. In this manner we can adjust the lighting blend from night-time (above) through dawn (below) and into bright midday hues, as desired. A wide clear sticky tape was then put over the top, as the strips had a habit of peeling off the shiny UPVC when warm.

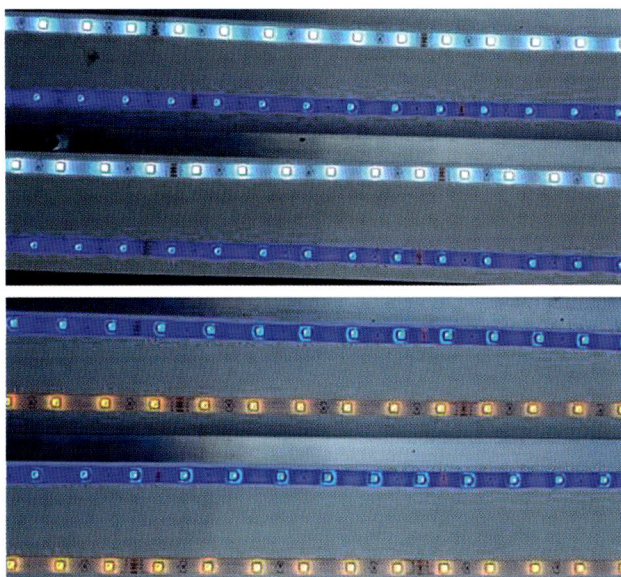

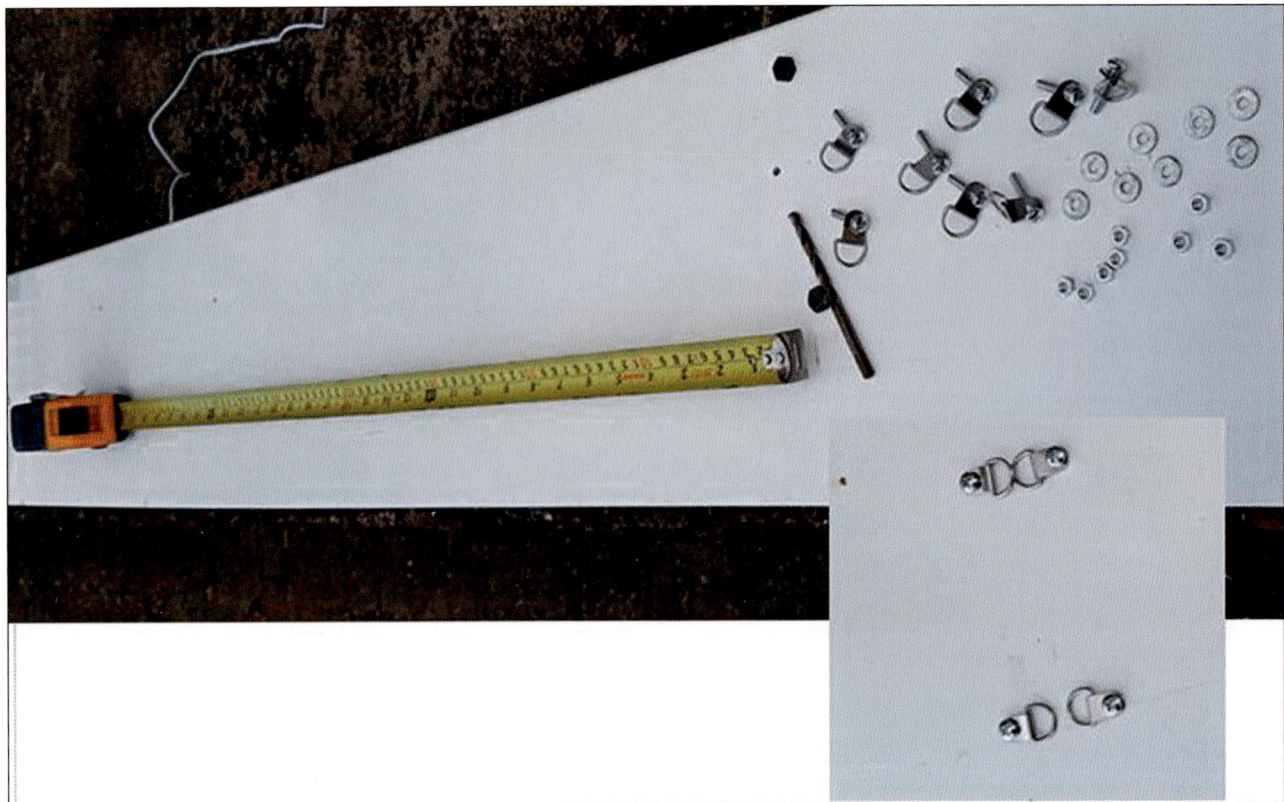

Small hangers were bolted into place to receive the cable ties used to hang the assembly from the lighting gantry. Ensure these go through the L girder to prevent warping.

The gantry set up in maintenance mode, maximum height. When constructing your layout, the best results come if the builder is both comfortable when working on it, and has an idea of the finished lighting effects desired. When operating the layout at exhibitions these gantry legs will be lowered by two holes, thus reducing the gap to the board by 8cm, and bringing in more concentrated light without dazzling the public. The lighting is adjusted via a remote control unit that came with the kit, hence there is a control box at either end to enable each LED array to be controlled independently when the remote control is pointed at it. This control box spacing meant that the low voltage supply cable had to be extended to reach a mains power source. The benefit of this is that the two transformer box plugs for the lighting are not hard-attached, being carried separately and not dangling from the rig in transit.

10
Buildings and Infrastructure

Lincoln Central Station, 7 August 1965. The clean lines of modern buildings are clearly visible behind Drewry works number 2680 0-6-0 DM shunter D2299, allocated 40A, which lasted just under ten years in BR service. Brick low-line post-war offices, steel clad factories and new blocks of flats are all springing up. Despite being a new railway model scale in the UK, the future is bright for TT:120 as well. Technology allows for swift lead time adaptations of existing designs of buildings. Card print on demand, laser cutting and 3D printing all provide alternatives that earlier modelling generations could only have dreamed of. (*Online Transport Archive: Meredith 605-4*)

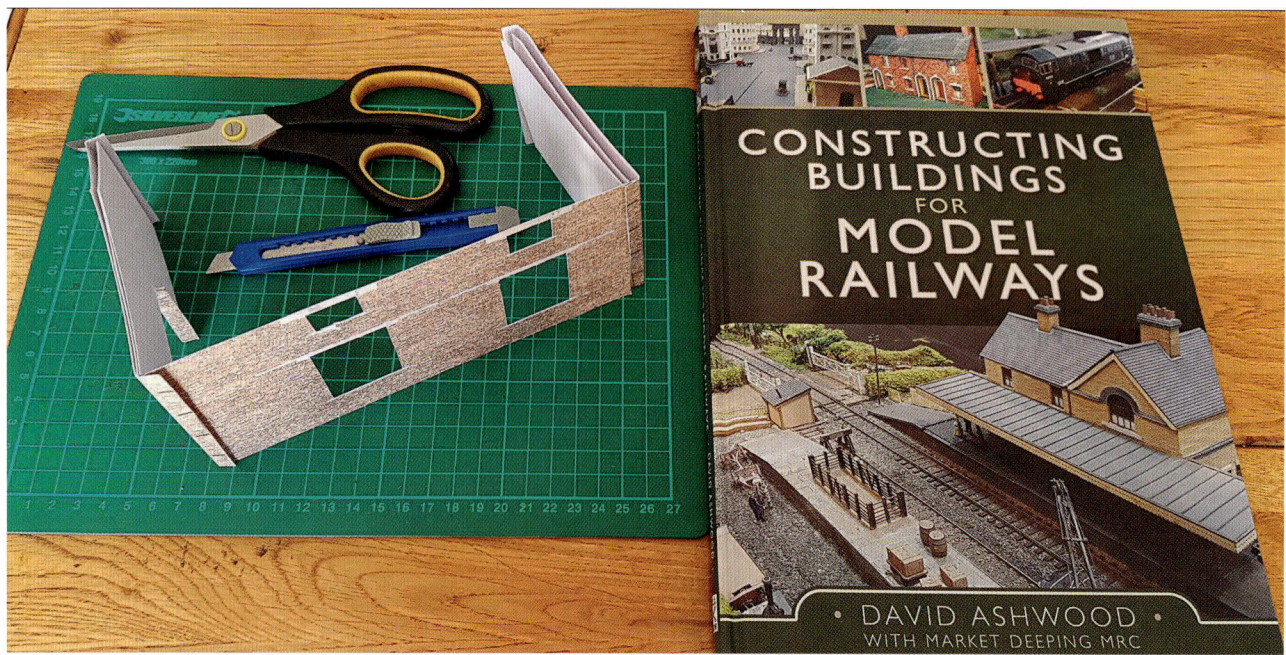

In this chapter, we focus specifically on buildings in TT:120. The Club has also produced a book dealing with model building construction in general (*Constructing Buildings for Model Railways*, Pen and Sword 2023), which covers techniques and materials in a variety of scales. The first worked example here is a downloaded 'print your own' warehouse kit from Scalescenes.com, which was provided free as a part of the initial TT:120 Club publication.

Initial glue work on the warehouse was undertaken outside for the purposes of ventilation. Permanent spray mounting adhesive was used to give fast grab without movement.

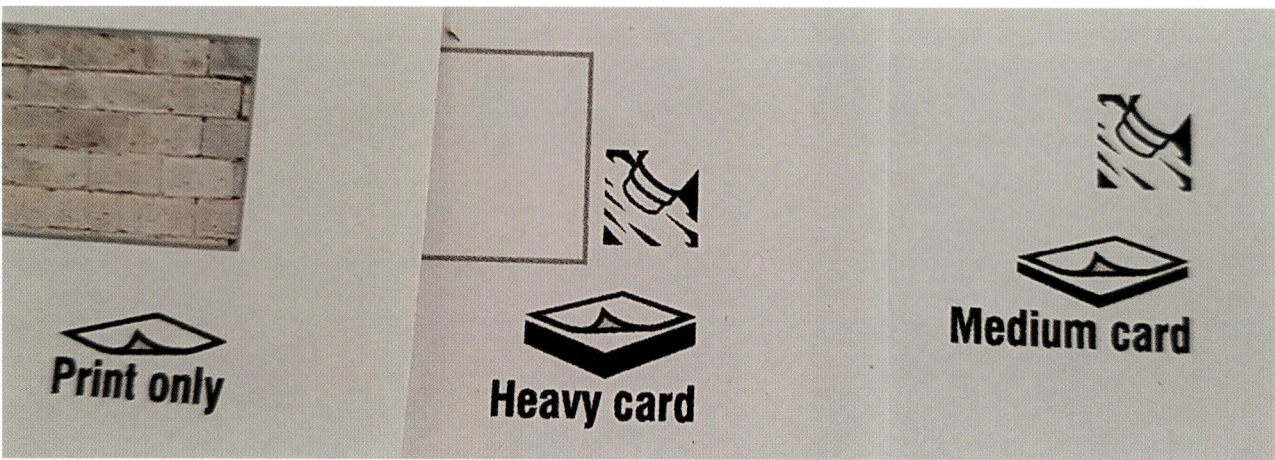

The individual sheets of printout require specific backing card weights. As a stock of postcard-weight material was available, multiple layers were glued together with PVA adhesive. This approximated to the light (110gsm) through heavy (1.5mm) weight requirement without having to invest in more card.

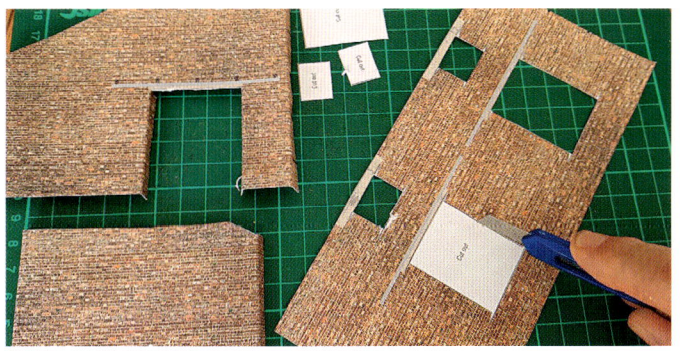 

Above left: Cutouts for windows and doors that would be pre-cut in a normal kit need to be made with a very sharp craft knife. They can be cut out freehand, or using a steel rule with finger protection. Always cut away from the fingers and body.

Above right: Rookie mistake: the blade had not been snapped off after becoming blunted on a previous model. The resulting pull and snag of the cover paper required some remedial work.

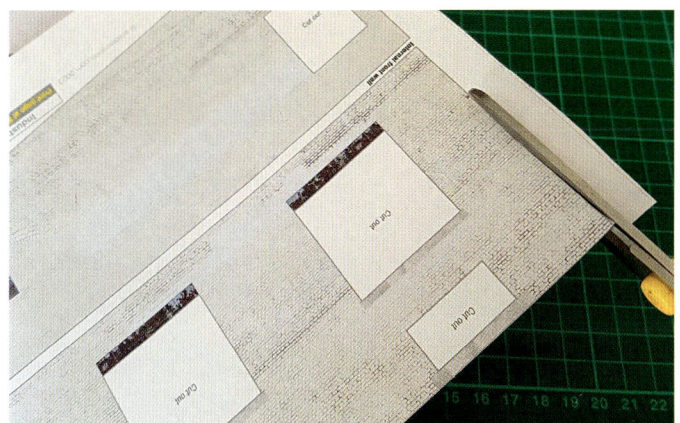

When cutting to size, have sharp paper scissors to hand to ensure a clean edge. These prints include interior detail with mirror-image cutouts to the external walls. Kits from downloads can be rescaled. A purchased OO scale kit could be adjusted to 63% on a printer to become a TT:120 kit. Upscaling is harder due to pixelation of the smaller source material.

As the kit begins to come together, the overall look and feel emerges. In TT:120 there is a degree of fiddly cutting and trimming, but certainly not a reflection of that involved for N gauge.

Kitchen-size matchsticks, short and long bamboo skewers. Both cheap alternatives to balsa wood ensure the constructed walls and roof are rigid.

The platform was reinforced by some spare artist's foamboard, which is lightweight and very rigid. The platforms tend to take some bumping on a model railway, so strength is important.

The finished warehouse goods platform. The laser printed brickwork has a good three-dimensional quality to it. The upper windows have a choice of glazing or plywood blanks, and the latter give a great feel of approaching dereliction.

Even the rear side of the building has great design in the angles and printing. Brick, paint and the plaster remains of removed extensions add to the feel.

Seen with a recently released BG coach in maroon livery, and a lightly modified box van to make it look like a load-sprung shocvan, the little goods warehouse facility will live at the back of the main running line on *Black Bridge*.

Mini Project: Teignmouth Bridges

On Saturday 31 March 1979 a down express behind 'Hoover' 50 016 *Barham* comes into Teignmouth station from the sea curve. For *Holcombe Beach* these two bridges mark the scenic end, leading to the fiddle yard. They were important to get correctly portrayed and many photographs were taken from the seafront looking towards these landmarks. The 'bailey bridge' style of the further East Cliff Walk bridge teetering on tall piers was a challenge in itself. (*Martin Addison CC BY-SA 2.0 Deed Geograph (truncated)*)

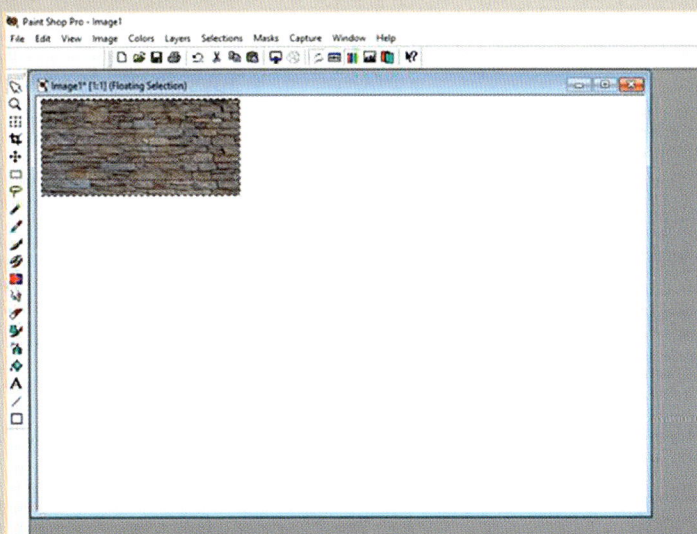

There are occasions when off-the-shelf accessories are not able to satisfy a requirement. In this case we were unable to locate any brick papers that a) fitted TT:120 scale well and b) were of the required colour and format. We needed tabular stones in the specific gentle mauve hue taken from the local 'freestone' rock formations. Fortunately, on a visit to Teignmouth an image was taken of a wall of this stone. The centre of the image was then isolated, to reduce lens distortion from a mobile phone photograph. This meant we were able to blend in multiple copies of this in a PC art package, taking us up to A4 sheet size. If your image contains shadows, always ensure you know which way is up, because the optical illusion of 3D jointing is important.

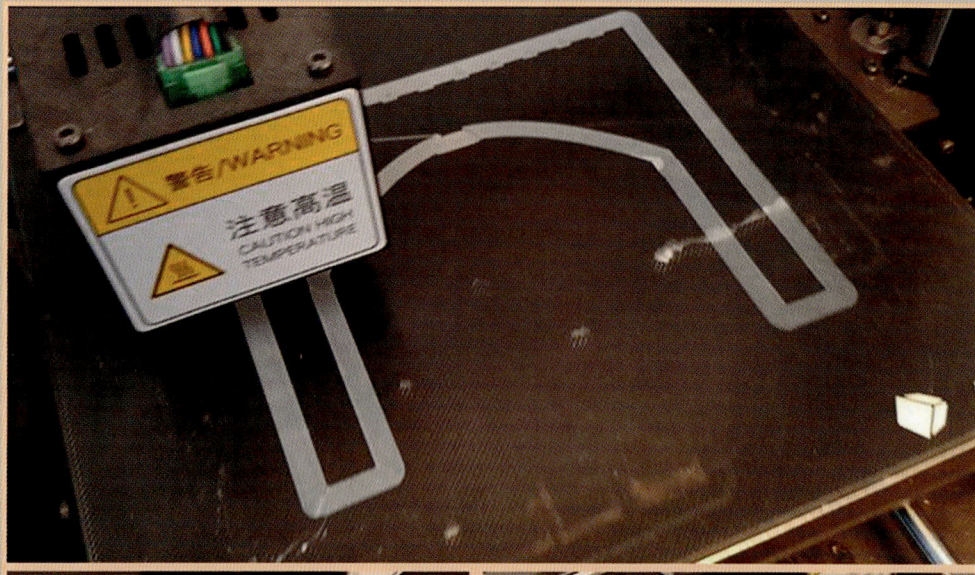

You can use balsa wood, card or foamboard as the basis for a model. In our case we decided on a mixed format, using a 3D-printed tunnel end that had been resized for the TT:120 road bridge. Thermally extruded plastics can create very strong objects, ideal for a scenic element that would be separately transported to an exhibition. You can see the multi-layer build-up as the hot extruder head passes over the 3D artefact.

The road bridge under construction. The printed paper is being adhered to the plastic and foamboard surfaces with a Bostic/UHU-type general clear glue. Retaining walls are steadied by being pierced by cocktail sticks until the glue sets.

Right: As with most freelance build projects, from an oil rig to a latticework bridge, it is all a question of working out components, sourcing them, and then putting them together meaningfully. A number of different 3D models can be sourced from https://www.thingiverse.com and are free to use. You get to know the components that go into each. Thus one can pick and choose, resizing on the PC printing tool as needed. This is a mix of components from an HO plate bridge, an O scale seaside pier and a OO factory, resized from original to TT:120 using https://www.modelbuildings.org/scale-to-scale-converter/.

Once glued into place, a basecoat suitable for the year portrayed was added. Today it's a nice glossy deep blue from a 2008 refurbishment when the stones were also sand blasted, but in the late 1980s it was a rusty weathered mid-green.

Below: Dry run. Looking good with the footbridge up on wooden offcuts, covered with the brick papers and having the keystones painted on the corners Then off to the Club, only to find the East Cliff Walk road bridge was 1cm too tight for the long HST Mark 3 C3 coaches on the curve. Lesson: don't just measure – offer up rolling stock as well.

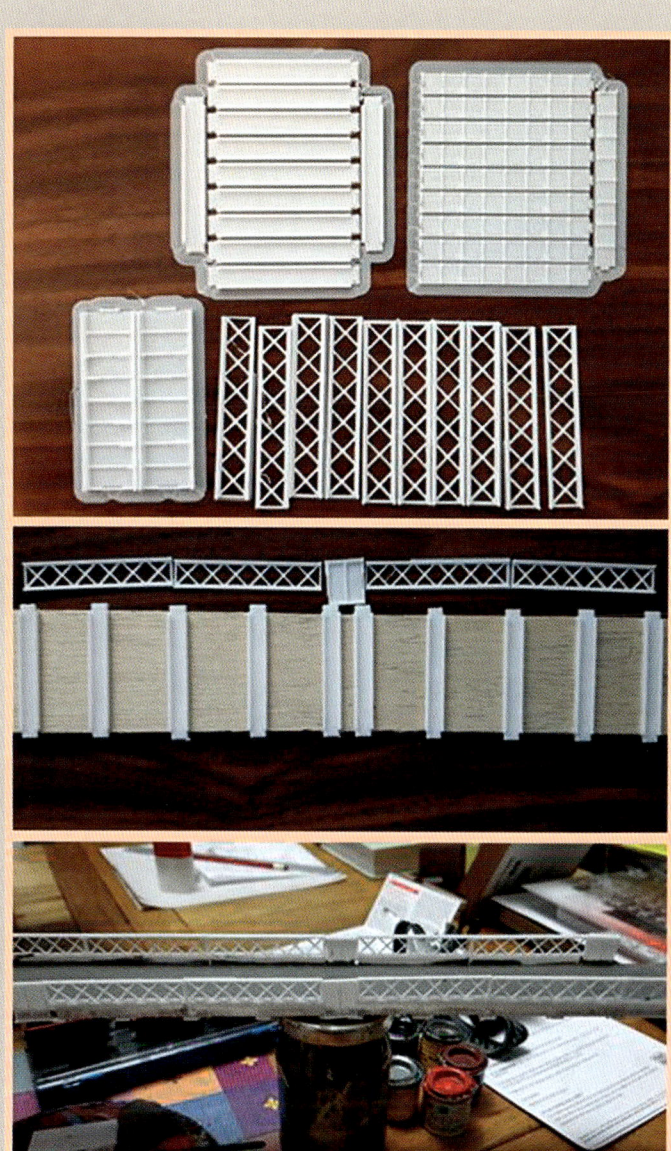

Left: A summer holiday season view of the prototype on 9 August 2011, showing the run into Teignmouth station from the sea wall. Small landslips are a way of life here, hence the low sleeper wall. (*Sarah Charlesworth CC BY-SA 2.0 Deed Geograph*)

Below: Norman Wisdom walking over the railway on the steep East Cliff Walk bridge in the 1966 film *Press For Time*. (*Rank Ltd*)

A view showing the bridges and detailed backscene for this corner, leading to Teignmouth station. The near roadway on East Cliff Walk has just been painted, hence the gloss look. The rear bridge is the Mark 2 version, printed to be 1cm wider. When the longer Mark 3 coaches were released, yet another bridge rebuild was required, with the aperture wider still to allow for the accentuated overlap on the curve. The opportunity was taken to use scribed plaster and paint the stonework. Printed stone sheets work well, but the station curve was being given much photographic scrutiny at shows, hence a more detailed finish was required.

BUILDINGS AND INFRASTRUCTURE • 97

The firm LCUT Creative has released a range of laser cut buildings in TT:120 scale, initially based on the east coast railway scene. We took the opportunity to purchase a couple, to both document the build and make good use of the end product. Our toolkit for these kits was a simple one:

a soft-cut self-healing craft mat or glass cutting board

a 'Stanley'-style knife with a new blade for the tough cutting

a snap-off type knife for smaller work and, with blade extended, used for any whittling that might be needed

a scalpel-style craft knife

a metal ruler

small sharp scissors

Bostik general glue (PVA or UHU can also be used).

Once the frets were checked, the instructions were read twice and annotated. Next, some painting was done in situ to get an undercoat in place. This can distort the materials when dry, so a heavy book should be used to flatten them later. With the 'Stanley', the walls were removed from the fret, and with scissors the window frames were coaxed out. Although the final colour of the building is not accurate at this point, the undercoating aids a decent adherence of topcoat and weathering at the end of process.

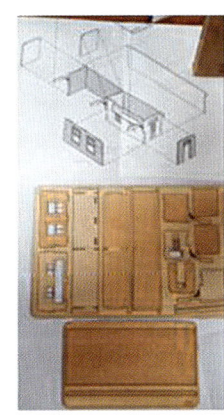

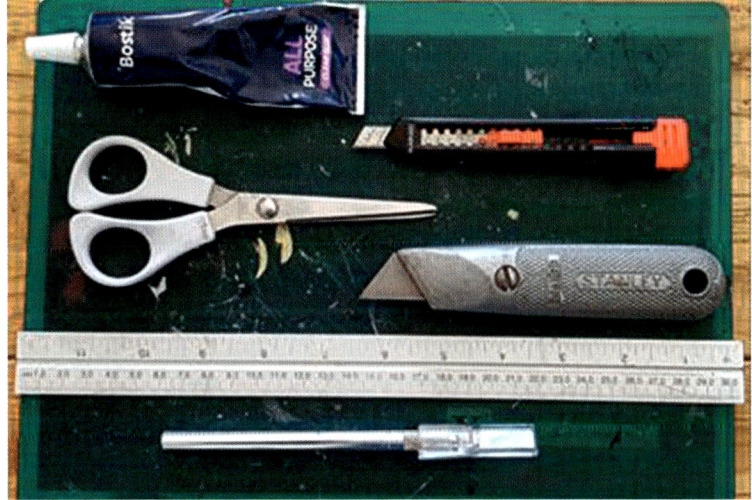

Several enamel paint coats were required to seal the surface of the laser embossed outer walls. As the building came together, extra coats were added. The bracing of the model ensured that paint warping of long walls did not occur.

Roof bracing with this thickness of material is essential. The LCUT kit comes with plenty, so no extra matchsticks or similar were required.

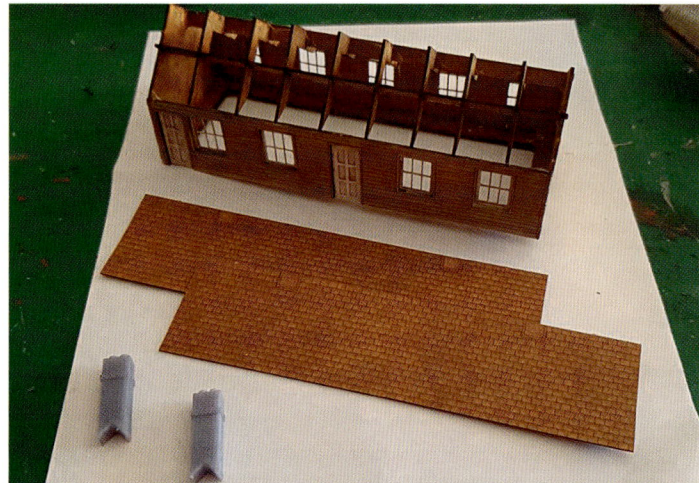

Once the roof trusses were in place, and with a final matt white enamel coat added to the frames, the glazing strips were added.

Final stage. This and several other contemporary buildings on the layout are being batched up for roof painting to ensure the same weathered hue is mixed and applied. Planning ahead can ensure a cohesive end result in a model town such as that on *Black Bridge*.

Mini Project: A Moving Roadway for Black Bridge

Right: An advertising example from the Club archive. Tri-ang Minic Motorways were released in the 1960s and designed to go side by side with the Tri-ang model railway system, broadening a model's infrastructure to embrace the roads. Minic Motorways used self-driven 1:76 scale OO models with a brass chassis and micro motor. Their three-pole motors were powered at 12V and were moved using piston-type controllers connected to the power take-off from the railway transformer. In common with the Scalextric racing sets they were powered by a metal-sided road slot. Technically the pickup was from rotating insulated brass wheels, rather than the steel braid of the racers.

Right, below left and below right: As a Club we had some experience with a moving roadway, as we used the Faller system on our South African railway project, *North Cape, Kimberley*. Faller's is a follow-the-wire type system, where a steel wire is placed under the roadway and self-powered vehicles follow the wire, auto steering as they go. If we only wanted buses and lorries moving in TT:120, then it may have been possible to scale things back. However the wheel sets, rechargeable power packs and charging points would not scale for normal cars. Back to square one.

The road system decided upon was that by Magnorail, purchased through a UK agent. Suitable for OO/HO, TT:120, N and Z, this system would take available vehicles in the scale: attach magnets, and away you go. As well as cars, buses and lorries, in OO/HO there is also the option of a pedalling cyclist. Maybe one day for TT:120.

The 'Expert' starter kit comes with just under a metre of guides, tracking and a 12V electric motor to drive it all. So long as a complete circle with medium radius curves was possible in the townscape, then moving vehicles were viable for *Black Bridge*.

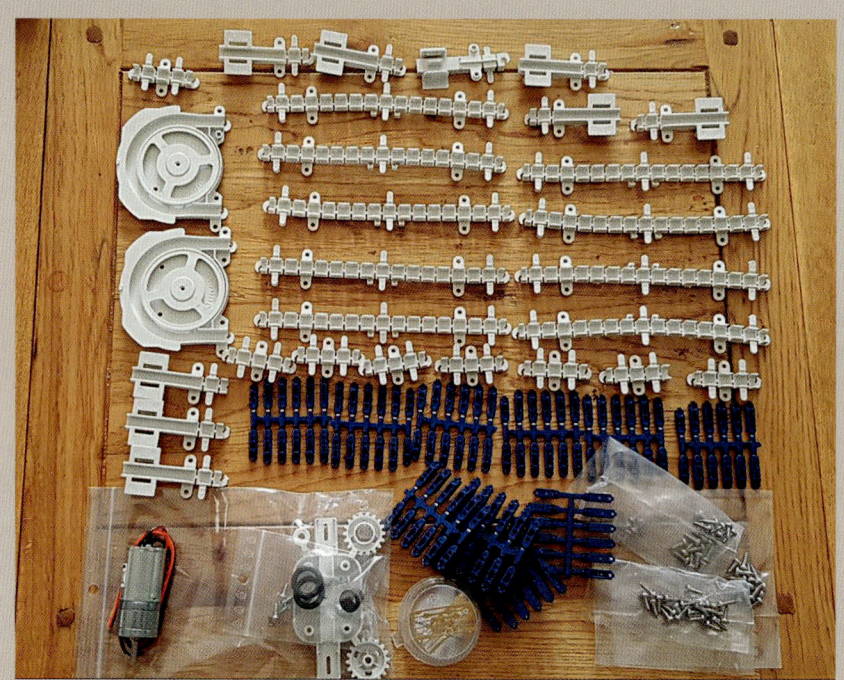

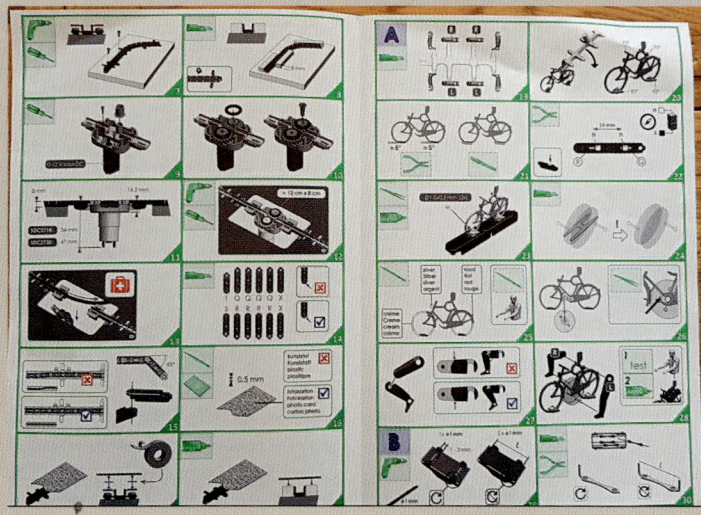

Many kits and systems purchased from abroad are annotated using the 'Ikea' method of pictograms. In common with them you sometimes do not know if a spare part at the end was an option or a requirement. A dry run is recommended wherever possible.

BUILDINGS AND INFRASTRUCTURE • 101

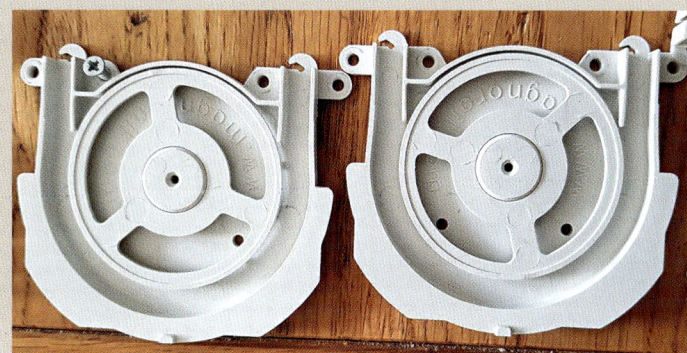

If tighter returns are needed, for example two-way traffic and a small roundabout, then two drive chain return wheels are provided.

The drive chain guides are of a nylon material, suitable for bending a few times in tests before they start to give under the strain.

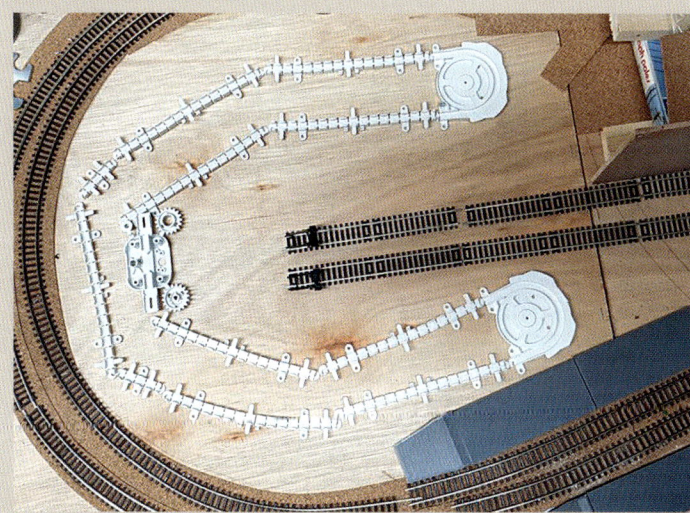

The main townscape is to the left of the layout and restricted to a single board, since the infinite loop drive chain is unsuitable for going over joints. Here we can see the first layout experiment. Station drive and roundabout with passing two-way traffic to the rear.

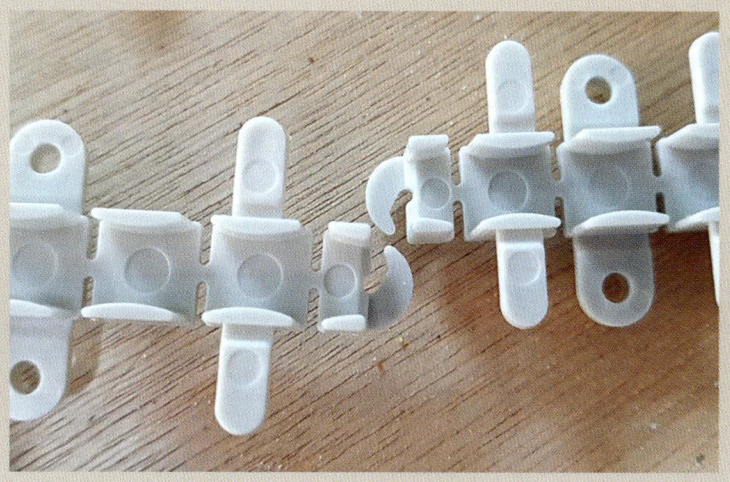

The guides are connected with a horizontal 'click to make' hook at each end. These can link a few times, but will give out quite quickly if you cannot make up your mind what is required.

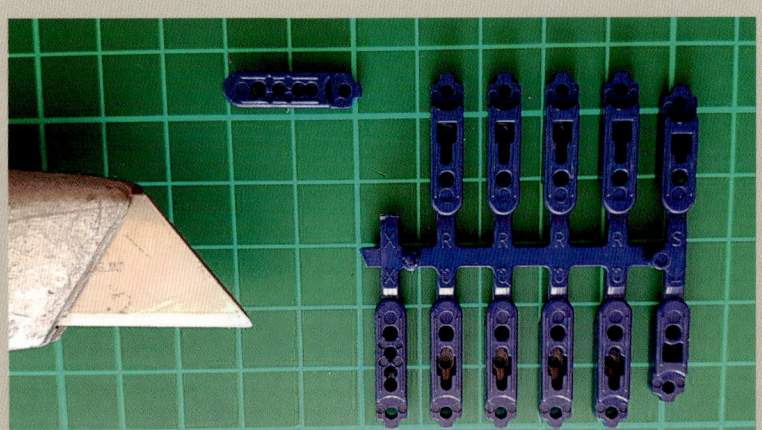

On a fret are the different drive chain segments. Adjusting numbers and length of these components will allow the continuous loop of the chain to be snug to the length of the guides used. The differing slots and circles are to accept rare earth magnets of one polarity to pull those of the opposite polarity on a vehicle slider shoe.

The chain sections have a clever peg and retainer setup. They are dropped in at 45° and on straightening they stay put. Once slotted into the guides, with a roadway on top, they will be in constant tension.

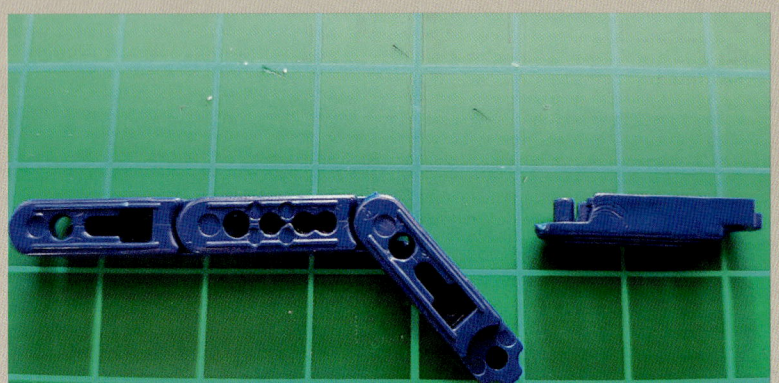

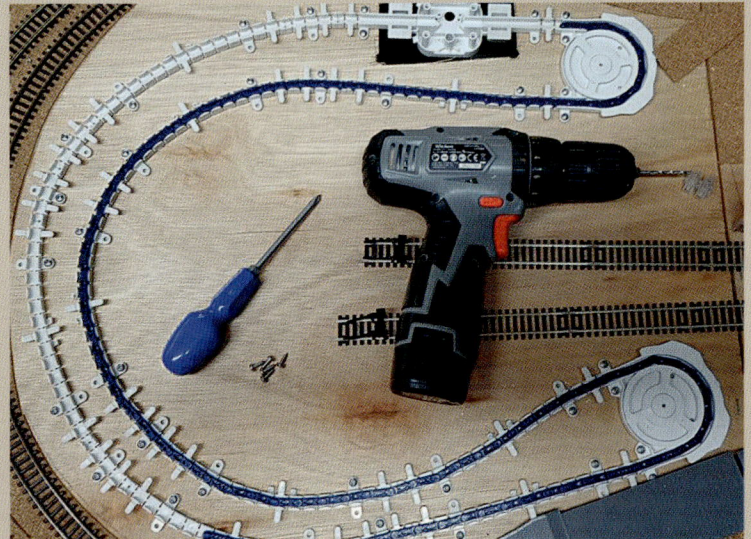

Once the track guide location and length is decided upon, it can be screwed into position. Screws are provided as a part of the kit.

The drive mechanism is a simple intermeshed gear with a rubber drive ring for the chain. A spare H&M 12V controller would be used to provide variable power. This we can have between a scale 5mph and a boy racer performing handbrake turns in the station car park.

BUILDINGS AND INFRASTRUCTURE • 103

Right: There are several ways of providing a roadway for the magnet running system. Due to friction causing eventual damage to magnet skates and wheels, sandpaper or wet and dry paper are best avoided as a road material. A plasticard roadway surface is an option but we decided to experiment with photographic paper or normal print paper, encapsulated. Thermal clear encapsulation gave a high gloss finish, but would be hard wearing. Based on the amount of use expected, the photo paper route was chosen. A photograph was taken of a typical road surface, which was then 'mosaiced' using a PC art package to form a larger print. Then panels were made up to cut out, with as few join lines as possible. With photographic papers it is important to keep finger contact to a minimum because skin oils will corrupt the print.

Below: More road surface was printed than was required to surface the main drive route. This was to allow a consistent look and feel with any other static roadway being created. The fire pump would become a static display vehicle as the turnarounds are too tight for realistic steering. The small vehicles run very smoothly. The chain drive at the rear is covered in clear plastic of the same thickness, allowing monitoring of the system, and access to drop the motor and rive out if needed. In the future we will be introducing levelling-up for building foundations using foamboard, plus some pavements to cover the road edges.

The Windmill

Above left, above right and left: Prior to the Industrial Revolution, post and tower windmills dominated the rural scene. The fact that many locations were consequently swallowed up by conurbations left the legacy of 'Mill Hills' and 'Mill Lanes' on wind-exposed areas throughout the land. An early memory of the TV interlude starring Pakenham Mill in Suffolk, turning on camera with the traditional corn stooks below, has stuck with the author for many years. Local to the Club is Heckington windmill which, with eight sails, dominates a manned level crossing. Could we model a TT:120 example for the rural side of *Black Bridge*?

Right: Inoxion Models 3D-printed resin model of a brick tower prototype to the rescue via an advert flashed up on Facebook. A great example of 'right place right time' advertising. The product is quick to market as the same model is rescaled and printed from a single computer model.

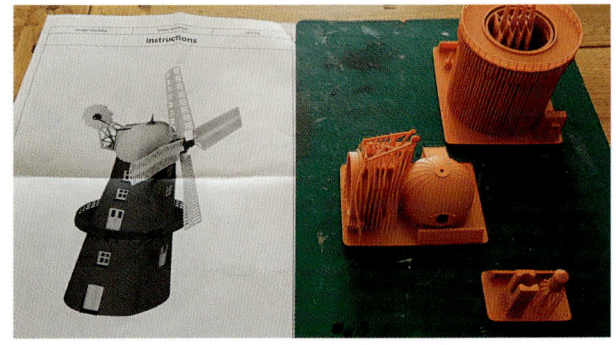

As delivered the model is seen to take good advantage of 3D printing methodology: an LED screen is situated in the base of a bath of resin, exposing light and fixing the material where light shows. Slowly lifting the print base out of the bath builds your object layer by layer. As a result the two rings of the windmill tower are printed like a 'Russian doll' and the sails protected inside that. Here the outer print support rods are being gently removed. They exist to prevent the balcony becoming 'droopy' before the resin has set.

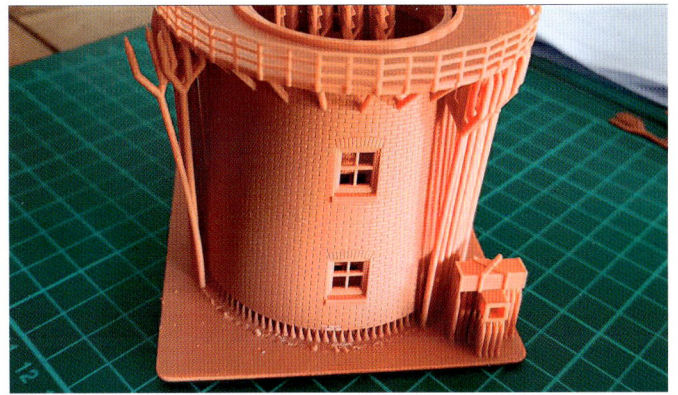

Delicate supports are pre-printed in place for the upper gallery walkway. As a modeller used to the 'old school' Airfix-style kits, this comes as both a relief and somewhat a disappointment in terms of missing out on a challenge.

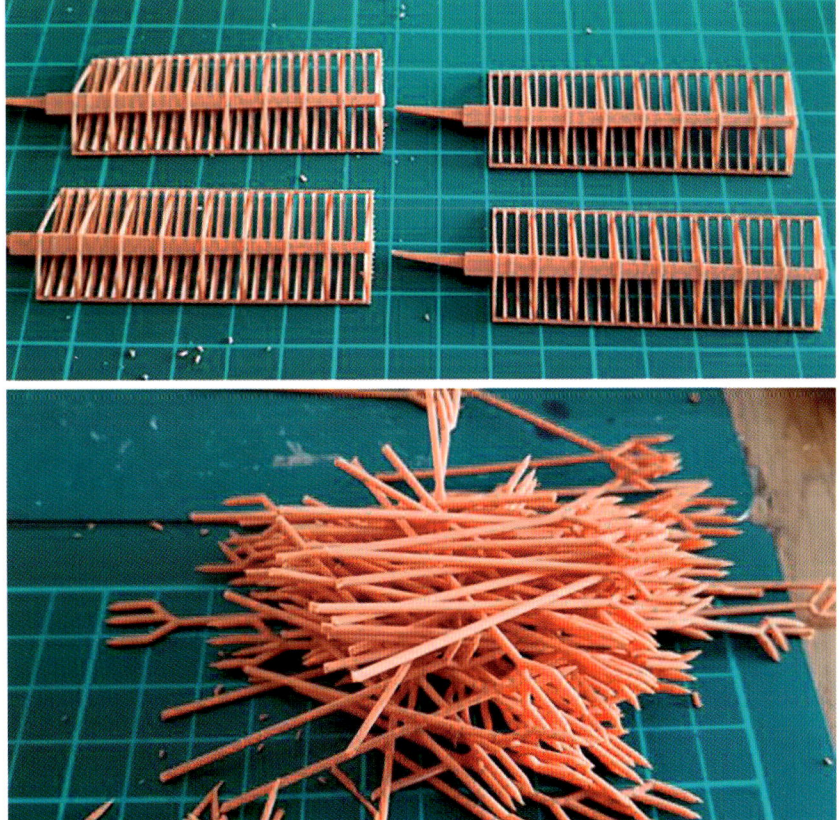

Above left: With the supporting sprues removed, the two rings with their detailed windows and brickwork can be dry assembled. Window frames were painted first. Then, with the aid of a cocktail stick, general purpose glue was used to adhere the glazing plastic into place.

Above right: The mill sails detached from the print base and ready for painting off-white. Meanwhile there is a big pile of offcuts to make into drain pipes and similar.

A thinned coat of 'Unbleached Linen' enamel paint as a base coat for the brickwork. London stock bricks would weather to dark brown from yellow, so weathering is due next. In County Durham these bricks would have been sold off from ship ballast in the returning colliers from the Port of London.

The sails are wonderfully delicate, while being fairly robust. There is however always the danger of a sharp knock fracturing them on the finished model. So rather than sticking the hub in place we plan to use a rubber bung, allowing it to be knocked off accidentally without damage.

Left and above: Alford, in central Lincolnshire. Research showed that this windmill was being rebuilt, so there was the ideal opportunity to photograph the cupola while craned onto the ground. We must not forget to build the miller's dwelling, and also the ancillary buildings for dry storage that clustered around the taller windmills.

This cottage, used as the miller's dwelling, was purchased as an outline CAD plan in TT:120 from an online source, and then resin 3D-printed at home by member Brian Norris. This means that such a model can be repeated if more are desired. Please remember to respect any print licence issued – they are there to keep our web 'friends' developing new examples, quick to market. Printing others' work for profit, or passing designs on, should be morally (and legally) avoided. See sites such as yeggi.com, cults3d.com or thingiverse.com for great examples.

Above: Inoxion Models came out with a 3D-printed TT:120 model of the Crooked House pub in South Staffordshire at the time of its controversial demolition. Although not in our region, we decided it was a worthy addition to the mill complex.

Right: It is often easier to put together different scenes as separate mini display boards, and then blend them into the main railway board. This means you can work at a desk, workbench or tabletop and not continually have to crane over the lines to the backscene. Here the three main buildings are stuck to a thin ply sub-board, and the base colours of the grounds are painted in with blended acrylic artist's paints.

So here is our completed sub-board. A mix of rough 2mm and autumn mix 2mm static grass has been dabbed onto brushed PVA adhesive. This is to keep the finished grass lower than it would be if a static grass applicator had been used. A small wall was erected, delimiting the pub from the houses, and Woodland Scenics underbrush bushes glued in. The yellow weeds are WWScenics OO daffodils. This board will be placed next to the NCB sidings on *Black Bridge*, mixing clean and dirty industries together.

On Creed, Ethnicity and the Built Environment

In our third book we did much to bemoan the lack of minority inclusion in the details of the models on display at exhibitions. Naturally, this will vary according to the date being portrayed, as well as the location, yet we were keen to make our layouts representative beyond the simple 'WASP' (white, Anglo-Saxon Protestant) appearance of people and, in terms of the subject of this chapter, buildings.

For the Devon coast in the late 1980s we could at least show a variety of visitors on the sea wall and beach. *Black Bridge* is set in the early 1950s, so more variety of places of worship were called for beyond the standard parish church, and an old Wesleyan hall will be placed in the town as well.

We would encourage you to look at populated images of your prototype area and date. You can gain an idea of what should be present for a realistic scene. Such subtle realism is often picked up by the external observer.

Above: A resin church in approximately 3mm scale was found on a second-hand stand at our annual show. Ideal for a little more detailing and positioning as part of a north-eastern town churchyard on *Black Bridge*. Alas there is no chance here of cheating with lighting windows and using decorative Christmas sticky tape as stained glass.

Below: Left: As we had a location in south-western England, a chance for a different form of worship! We scratchbuilt a model of the Corinthian Yacht Club, which occupies a landmark building on East Cliff Walk at the junction of the railway and the bridges. This appears in so many photographs of the railway that it was worth using 'modeller's licence' to shift it a little to the east from its true location. *Right*: Politeness. Dawlish/Holcombe is a family holiday spot, so we made sure all the bathers were well covered.

In the early 'noughties' of this century, back in South Ealing, the author used to send numerous models via the local sub post office. This was run by a couple who were always having to put their own money in to balance the books with the new computer system. Now, with the Post Office computer scandal exposed, it is time for Swati and her husband to have a nice holiday away from the pressures of business. They can be found on the Devon shore at Sprey Point …

11
In Retrospect: Hornby Dublo vs TT:120

Feeling rather like an early TT:120 or indeed original Hornby Dublo station: packed full of promise, but still with a perceived long wait for fulfilment. This is Blackpool North in 1966. Without holiday specials being run to capacity, the normal DMU services appear to hide in the corners of the terminus. Class 24 D5001 sits ticking over with a minimal parcels consist on the photographer's platform. *(BR (M) Derby)*

TT:120 is not the first time Hornby has been involved with a change in scale and market-leading innovation. The Hornby Dublo product holds a special place in the heart of older modellers, the foundation dating back to autumn 1938.

Hornby Dublo was launched in that year by the British company Meccano Ltd of Binns Road

An example of a post-1953 Hornby Dublo catalogue. The locos, carriages, tankers and brake van are all familiar as early TT:120 releases today.

Liverpool, owners of Frank Hornby's original model railway assets. They had already produced larger O gauge tinplate clockwork and latterly electric powered trains. Dublo was introduced as a response to the demand for smaller, OO gauge model trains and represented the first steps into the smaller scale by the company.

This is where parallels with the launch of TT:120 can be drawn: a step into a new scale with an uncertain market, a release schedule upset by international events, a number of naysayers in the media. The initial Dublo offerings were a limited portfolio of rolling stock, track and scenic items, concentration being upon the ready-to-run boxed set. For the time, the detail, quality and robustness of the product were noteworthy. The initial products included a clockwork entry-level set and a simple electric boxed set with passenger or freight operating as a three rail system (the central rail was live and the running rails a common return).

Despite its popularity and reputation for quality, Hornby Dublo struggled to compete with emerging trends and changing consumer preferences in the 1960s. In 1964, Meccano was acquired by Lines Bros, which eventually phased out the Hornby Dublo brand in favour of their own Tri-ang Railways line. Production of Hornby Dublo ceased in 1964, marking the end of an era.

The original table-top Hornby Dublo railway with one of our previous books for scale. Tinplate three-rail track, tinplate litho-printed carriages and a heavy die-cast locomotive. The scale would fit onto a large extended table and layouts were easy to construct. Dublo was robust and good for unattended play.

TT:120 with plastic sleeper two-rail lighter-weight track, injection moulded carriages and a well detailed locomotive. This scale fits onto a smaller tabletop in line with modern housing. With a higher price point, especially if chipped, and an inherent fragility, attended play of younger family members is a must.

Why we 'do' model railways ... whether as individuals or members of a club, the model railway fraternity treat modelling and consequent operation as a means to relax. Those zen moments are much needed in life, as are the good feelings of accomplishment. Here members Mick, Bill and Alan relax with the completed TT:120 *Holcombe Beach* on display at a local show, as a final train of the day 'bimbles' home to the depot alongside a stormy sea.